RAINMAKER CONFIDENTIAL

HOW TOP PROFESSIONALS MAKE SMART BUSINESS DEVELOPMENT INVESTMENTS OF TIME, TREASURE, AND TALENT

Henry DeVries, Scott Love & Mark LeBlanc

INDIE BOOKS
INTERNATIONAL®

BookBlueprint™, BookChat™, and BookKickoff™ are pending trademarks of Indie Books International, Inc.

Client Attraction Chain Reaction™ is a pending trademark of Henry DeVries.

Defining Statement™ is a pending trademark of Mark LeBlanc.

Growing Your Business™ is a pending trademark of Mark LeBlanc.

Indie Books International® is a registered trademark of Indie Books International, Inc.

Marketing With A Book™ is a pending trademark of Henry DeVries.

Persuade With A Story™ is a pending trademark of Henry DeVries.

Rainmaker Retreat™ is a pending trademark of Henry DeVries, Scott Love, and Mark LeBlanc.

ISBN-13: 978-1-952233-77-7
Library of Congress Control Number: 2021948090

Designed by Joni McPherson, mcphersongraphics.com

INDIE BOOKS INTERNATIONAL®, INC
2424 VISTA WAY, SUITE 316
OCEANSIDE, CA 92054

www.indiebooksintl.com

DEDICATION

*To our rainmaking
mentors, who gave so
generously of their wit
and wisdom.*

Tim,

Best of luck to
you!

CONTENTS

FOREWORD

In business, it's all about who you know and cultivating those relationships. For some, these connections come naturally and then there are *the rainmakers*. They are the people that, almost like magic, bring in new business, new accounts, and new revenue. That's a talent not everyone has, but it's something that can be cultivated.

We all have a set of talents and it's our responsibility as leaders to zero-in on those talents and use them to amplify our success and that of our teams. Let's call that our competitive advantage. Every company has their own rainmaker, so how do we stand out and make it rain harder on our end?

The first step is simple—adapt! It's all about being nimble enough to adapt to a new set of rules. Instead of eyeballs and ears, the new game involves hearts and minds. It's about quality over quantity. While it's great to have many eyeballs on you, your brand, or your business, all your customers will remember is how they felt after interacting with you and how you helped them solve their problems.

The second step is being authentic every step of the way. If you're just trying to sell someone your latest product, without making a connection, you're not going anywhere. Customers are savvy enough to see phony coming from a mile away. No one wants to do business with someone who only sees dollar signs with every customer. Make it an experience, not a hard sell. That's the fastest way to turn someone off.

We live in an era that has enhanced the overall customer experience. They are who we need to please all the time. That's non-negotiable. The customization they're demanding is not something that will go away any time soon. Profits are great, but it's all about the customer. Using your time, talent, and treasure—or the three T's—to create an unforgettable experience is what we all need to use. The profits will come, and your CFO will be happy, but you must make that investment upfront—and it's not just a financial investment, but an emotional one too.

Once those clients feel like you understand their pain point(s) and try to engage with them, you must do everything in your power to retain them. Profits are more than just money. They can be measured in loyalty and the business that will generate for you.

This book provides a compilation of some key best practices, or "secrets," to help you become the best problem solver for your clients. Henry, Scott, and Mark provide readers with an actionable and timeless game plan to become the quintessential rainmaker and a trusted partner to each and every customer.

The forecast may call for rain, but it's always sunny when the client is happy.

Jeffrey Hayzlett
Primetime TV And Podcast Host
Chairman And CEO, C-Suite Network
Keynote Speaker, Bestselling Author, And Global Business Celebrity

PART I

WHY IMPROVING YOUR YOUR RAINMAKING MATTERS

SECRET #1

Why Not Compare Yourself To Successful Peers?

You cannot ask your most successful competitors and peers their secrets of rainmaking. That would be awkward, impractical, and sometimes illegal.

So, we did it for you. We went behind closed doors and asked the tough questions. We asked more than one hundred successful rainmakers what they are investing more in, what they are cutting back on, and what are their go-to strategies. In other words, how are they investing their time, treasure, and talent? Think of us as your rainmaking R&D department.

You've no doubt heard of using OPM (other people's money) to grow your business. This book is about using OPE (other professionals' experience) to grow your business.

This book is for those who serve in roles such as chief executive officer, general manager, principal, partner, or head of an office, business unit, or practice for professional service firms, especially in the fields of accounting, dental consulting, financial services, management consulting, marketing and advertising, executive search services, software development, technology services, and law firm management.

Some define R&D as research and development; we define it as rob and duplicate.

We have done the research so you can rob and duplicate the most successful rainmaking strategies from your professional peers. It's okay; we did not use espionage to gain their secrets. The OPE rainmaking insider secrets were willingly shared.

Some Say It Is All About Caring

There is a dangerous common misperception in rainmaking that goes something like this: "People don't care how much you know until they know how much you care."

Wrong-oh.

If you cling to this phrase as the basis of your rainmaking philosophy, you are making a gross miscalculation.

If you think you can win more high-paying clients by building better relationships, you are only partly correct. You make it rain by bringing value and contribution to your client.

The best way to win the hearts and minds plus loyalty of a client is to deliver value to them first, and let the relationship develop from there. If you focus just on building a relationship and neglect to solve a problem for your prospect, then you might end up becoming good friends with your prospect. And then you can watch how he will buy from your best competitor because your competitor showed how they could solve your client's problem.

MAKE IT RAIN

 Here are three rainmaking steps to take to better understand prospects:

First, find out what motivates the prospect to buy. This is done by asking questions. When discussing the issue, ask your prospect this question: "What problem would you be able to solve if my service achieves what we discussed?" If you can identify the problem, you can get the client.

Second, once you identify the problem, focus on that issue. This is the nerve that you must expose and as it is a sensitive issue, know that this is where the response will come from. Do it with delicacy, by saying something like this: "What would happen if you went six months and didn't solve that issue?" Ouch. This leads to pain which stimulates the motivation to act. It then becomes a compelling reason to act.

Third, bring closure to this line of question-asking by saying this: "So it sounds like with the addition of this service, you might be able to solve that issue, once and for all, right?" "Sure," they respond. Then say this: "So how does that affect your ability—for you personally—to perform?" The whole point is to bring it to the personal level. Find out how your service can solve an issue at the personal level in the mind of the high-level decision-maker.

Remember that people make decisions on an emotional and a personal level, and if you can find out how to solve a problem that affects that senior-level decision-maker on a personal level, you not only will get the business, you will have a friend for life. And that is the real secret to developing long-term relationships.

The real rainmaking truth: People do not care how much you know until they know how much you can solve their problems.

Do The Math For The Client To Land The Deal

Did you hate word problems in math class back in school? Trust us; your clients hate word problems too, and that might just be what is hurting your closing rate.

"If a client was truly certain that hiring you would bring them a hefty ROI, they would hire you every time," advises copywriting expert Stefan Georgi. "That's why I recommend doing the math for a client."

Georgi, a direct response copywriter whose work has led to over $700 million in sales, knows how to sell a product, especially his own services.

Doing the math for the client is as straightforward as it sounds, and Georgi illustrated with an example.

"Say you want to charge a client $50,000 for a marketing campaign. You find out that their revenue goal is $1 million, and that their profit margin is roughly 20 percent. That means if the client hits their goal, they will net $200,000, which is a 4x return on what they paid you."

Spell that all out for the prospective client. "Then tell them that given your record of helping similar clients get results like these, you feel confident you can help them do the same thing," says Georgi.

Georgi says to show the client exactly what you can do for them. Whether that is through hard data, or a portfolio of success, or taking the initiative with spec work, there are a variety of ways to show those high-paying clients that you're the perfect fit for their business.

"When trying to land dream clients you run into two big obstacles: one, they don't know who you are, and two, they don't know if hiring you is going to yield a positive ROI," he notes. "You can alleviate both roadblocks by proactively providing the client with an immediately usable asset for free."

For example, a copywriter could reach out to a brand with a prewritten promotional email.

"Tell them you're a fan of their company, and since you're a copywriter, you decided to do an email for them for free (no strings attached)," says Georgi. "All you ask is they let you know how it performs. This strategy works because it gets you on the client's radar, differentiates you from the competition, and makes it easy for the client to see how working with you could yield a positive ROI."

For your future it is imperative to get data on performance. Provide useful numbers to prospects with measurable results testimonials, where the client mentions a raw number, percentage increase, or time savings.

"Make sure you are getting data and feedback from current clients," says Georgi. "That way, when talking to new prospects, you can leverage that data. Specifically, you can show the new prospect how you worked with a similar business in the past and got them excellent results. This increases your credibility and authority in that prospect's eyes."

Do not take any work just to pay the bills. Focus on going after clients who will make your work visible.

"The best clients and companies to work for are the ones who are already winning," says Georgi. "The reason why is because their processes are more dialed-in, which means your work is more likely to see the light of day. Once your work goes live you can point to the client, and the asset you created for them, when talking to similar prospects."

Georgi currently is a coach for business owners on copywriting and strategy as part of the Copy Accelerator company he cofounded.

Why You Must Measure Rainmaking ROI

When it comes to marketing return on investment, consider the words of Lord Kelvin, the British mathematical physicist from a century ago:

> *When you can measure what you are speaking about, and express it in numbers, you know something about it; but when you cannot measure it, when you cannot express it in numbers, your knowledge is of a meager and unsatisfactory kind.*

Is your knowledge of your marketing return on investment of a meager and unsatisfactory kind?

"Why do CFOs want to slap marketers in their face?" asks international marketing expert Pablo Turletti. "Is it because they cannot prove marketing investment returns?"

Turletti's metaphor conjures up ancient codes of conduct where you might get slapped as a challenge to your honor. Now, we do not condone duels or C-Suite face slapping, but Turletti has a point.

For those who want to attract high-paying clients, measurable results are imperative. Marketing leaders who claim that marketing cannot really be measured are frustrating to other business leaders. For marketing to become impactful to companies' bottom lines, Turletti advocates that marketing leaders need to start speaking the language of business. That language talks about return on investment.

MAKE IT RAIN

 What can rainmakers do to avoid the slap? Turletti offers several recommendations:

Include business objectives as part of marketing projects. "Measuring click-through rates (CTR), clicks, reputation, and awareness is not enough," says Turletti. "It is imperative to incorporate real economic credible indicators such as revenue and return."

Create your own attribution model. "There is not an off-the-shelf one," says Turletti. "You must create it using quantitative research, for your product or service, in your market. Forget about time decay, first or last click. These are arbitrary, nonrobust attribution models that can only prove that there are no criteria to isolate the economic impact of a project or campaign."

Go beyond profits internally. "Communication is at the core of all marketing activities," says Turletti. "Using this set of skills can transform the organization from the inside, incorporating social and environmental impact as part of the overall business plan. It is not about corporate social responsibility, but about corporate social business. The companies that will thrive in the future are the ones that will go beyond profits. It is essential that doing good to society and the environment becomes profitable, hence sustainable, and impactful—rather than rhetoric or esthetic."

Go beyond profits externally. "Marketing must deliver messages that reflect not only the functional or emotional characteristics of a product or service but its impact on a given purpose society can align with that is part of the business core," says Turletti. "At the same time, campaigns shall educate consumers around the idea that doing good and making money are not incompatible. Profitability and sustainability must go hand in hand."

Measure, measure, measure. "As Peter Drucker would say: you can only improve what you measure," says Turletti. "Measuring the actual return on marketing investments is key to show marketing's contribution to the bottom line of companies, to prove that sustainability can be profitable (and that there is nothing bad in it), making marketing and the company accountable not only to shareholders but to all stakeholders."

Turletti has worked in more than thirty countries for more than fifty multinational corporations, has written three books, teaches in two business schools, and hosts around forty conferences on marketing ROI per year.

The bottom line: To avoid the potential slap from CFOs, marketers must make sure they plan and work as a profit center and drive the business beyond those profits they measure.

Now on to the conclusions of our research, by sharing how the best rainmakers are investing their time, treasure, and talent.

"I appreciate all the trouble you've taken to
keep our appointment, but I'm not
with Technomaxx anymore."

SECRET #2

How The Best Rainmakers Invest Their Time, Treasure, And Talent

W hat are the secrets of top rainmakers? As we interviewed them, they shared this truth: the typical hype that works for retail products and low-cost services is not only a waste of time and money for consultants and professionals, but it also actually makes them less attractive to prospective clients.

When coauthor Henry DeVries wrote his bestseller *How To Close A Deal Like Warren Buffett*[1] with Tom Searcy, he discovered how Buffett uses stories to persuade, gain positive media coverage, and build a world-famous personal brand. In his weekly column on business development for Forbes.com, he saw how most professionals and consultants talk about their work in the same drab way. You cannot bore prospects into buying.

To attract new clients, the best business development approach for consultants and professionals is to demonstrate expertise by sharing valuable information through writing and speaking.

MAKE IT RAIN

 By Henry DeVries

The number one rainmaking tool is a book, and the number one rainmaking strategy is speaking. Research shows independent consultants and professionals can fill a pipeline with qualified prospects in as little as thirty days by offering advice to prospects on how to overcome their most pressing problems. From our research, here are the magnificent seven ways rainmakers parlay a book, listed in reverse rank order of return on investment (ROI) of time, treasure, and talent:

7. **Host paid workshops.** This is the strategy of renting out the ballroom at the local Marriott or Hilton and charging for an all-day or half-day workshop. Participants should take away a substantial packet of good information from your firm (and a good meal too). Coauthor Henry DeVries offers "Marketing With A Book And Speech" summits at no cost, and makes them invitation only. Those attending are paying with their precious time.

6. **Follow an internet game plan.** Send out weekly tips, blog weekly, and post articles on other blog sites and websites. Announce your blog posts and articles on social media (Twitter, LinkedIn, and Facebook are a must). This is the water-drip-torture school of marketing and the opposite of spam. By signing up for

your newsletter lists, prospects are telling you that they are interested in what you have to say, but are not ready for a relationship now. These people should receive valuable how-to information and event invitations from you on a monthly basis until they decide to opt out of the list. Have a YouTube channel and post new content on a monthly basis.

5. **Network at meetings and trade shows.** This is an excellent way to gather business cards and ask for permission to include them on your e-newsletter list.

4. **Get involved in community and association organizations.** Everyone likes to do business with people they know, like, and trust. You need to get involved and "circulate to percolate," as one Ohio State University professor used to say. Find the associations that are target-rich environments and volunteer to help.

3. **Get published with how-to articles in a client-oriented press.** Better than any brochure is the how-to article that appears in a publication that your target clients read.

2. **Give how-to speeches at client industry meetings.** People want to hire experts, and an expert by definition is someone who is invited to speak. Actively seek out forums to speak and list past and future speaking dates on your website.

1. **Host no-cost or low-cost small-scale seminars.** The best proactive tactic you can employ is to regularly

invite prospects by LinkedIn, snail mail, and email to small seminars or group consultations. If your prospects are spread out geographically, you can do these briefings via Zoom or the telephone using a bridge line (teleseminars). These can't be ninety-minute commercials. You need to present valuable information about how to solve the problems that your prospects are facing, and then just a little mention about your services. Offer all attendees a no-cost, no-selling, no-kidding follow-up strategy call.

The smart rainmakers have learned how to use writing and speaking to create a client attraction chain reaction.

Back in science class everyone learned that a chain reaction is a sequence of reactions that causes additional reactions to take place. In nuclear physics, what happens to a single neutron can result in a nuclear explosion. That applied science in 1942 under the bleachers at the University of Chicago and then in the desert of New Mexico was a game changer for science. We hope applying the research in this book will be a game changer for your rainmaking.

In these uncertain times, there is something all businesses need: more clients. Many rainmakers are searching for ways to connect with clients and become influential during the new business reality.

Sure, there are big winners during the pandemic such as Zoom, LinkedIn, and toilet paper companies. However, there are opportunities for most professionals and consultants if they pivot strategies.

"We are really learning to navigate this online Zoom reality that we're in and figuring it out for our clients," says Jean Freeman, principal and CEO of Zambezi, a Culver City, California based firm, which is the largest female-owned advertising agency in America. "We're advising our clients, from a business development standpoint, now is the time to really look at new types of targets and assess the viability of reaching new consumers, because consumer behavior is changing so drastically."

None of the successful rainmakers in our study suggested to just hunker down and hope the pandemic blows over.

"Now's the time to really look at opportunities in the market and a fully funded and aggressive approach to business development is a big part of that," says Emily Borders, cofounder and coprincipal of Highwire Public Relations of San Francisco.

Borders has looked hard at connecting with prospects through virtual events. "Clearly we're not getting on a plane anytime soon."

Borders's target industries, healthcare and technology, have been driven by events that are not happening in any of the ways they did before.

"We're really exploring how to connect virtually with our prospects, how we can make the most of virtual events, and helping our clients navigate that in the same way," adds Borders.

Because industry events are going virtual, rainmakers are having to adjust tactics to attract prospects and cement client relationships. Gone are the days of just showing up and networking your way to success.

"That means getting in there early, offering insights, building those personal and individual connections, not just on the day of the virtual event, but leading up to and around, and then after those virtual activations," says Borders. "And that will likely be a focus through at least the next year."

The new reality requires new strategies. For example, random sponsorships are out, says Chad Hetherington, CEO of The Stable, a consumer brand agency with offices in Minneapolis, Seattle, and Austin, Texas.

"We've just been a lot more strategic as it relates to how we allocate dollars in terms of our overall company business development strategy," says Hetherington. "So that's limited our costs and spending as well there."

A common theme from the rainmakers was to get better at using visual tools like Zoom.

"The pandemic has necessitated us being creative and increasing our ways to use Zoom and every other platform available to stimulate community engagement and outreach and make people feel that their voice in a process is still available when it's not necessarily in person," said Derek Danziger, president of the San Diego public relations firm Katz & Associates.

For years, Danziger has done a great deal of media crisis training for clients.

"One of the things I never trained about was the potential of a global pandemic happening," says Danziger. "It was the one thing that was not on my crisis list. And I need to adjust that now."

Four Ways To Attract Ideal Clients By Becoming A Trusted Authority

How can you position yourself as a trusted authority to your ideal prospects?

Scott Cantrell, who says his clients have generated more than $100 million of additional revenues by becoming trusted authorities, believes the answer comes down to three words: "Insight inspires influence."

To help clients have more influence and insight, Cantrell and his firm Smart Solutions Media work with business owners and professionals who want to attract high-value prospects and acquire more profitable clients by positioning themselves as trusted authorities.

"If you want to have a position of preeminence and become a trusted authority, then you must share your insights, and they must be clear, compelling, and consistent," says Cantrell.

Trusted authorities who consistently provide insight into the marketplace affirm the need (and desire) to hear from them, follow them, learn from them, and work with them.

MAKE IT RAIN

 Below are four actionable strategies Cantrell advocates that can position a consultant or professional as a trusted authority:

Maximize your visibility via value. "The first step to attracting high-value clients is consistently accessing and engaging the right decision makers. However, the goal should not merely be awareness but attention. By consistently and freely sharing meaningful value in the form of content like infographics, tools, and videos, over time, you will naturally be seen by your prospective clients as a true thought leader."

Leverage the power of a passionate point-of-view. "Don't be afraid to have an opinion and stick to it. Of course, it must make sense and you must be able to defend your position, especially if it is contrarian. By strategically establishing a clear, well-defined, and compelling philosophy, you will automatically attract decision makers who share or are fascinated by that specific point of view."

Show off your skills. "Authority comes from the demonstration of your knowledge, your skill, and your ability to get meaningful results for those you serve. The more people who experience your ability to help them, the more who will become clients. Consider how your product, service, or solution can best be experienced by a prospect; then deliver those demonstrations, letting them take away meaningful value before they ever formally become a client."

Deliver memorable methodology. "Not your product, service, or solution, but rather your methodology is your single most sustainable competitive advantage. Develop and name your own approach. Next, create a short assessment process for potential clients that naturally leads them to two conclusions: they need help and you're the one to provide that help."

What Cantrell calls memorable methodology we call proprietary process. Based on interviews with successful client rainmakers, it is a game changer.

Nashville-based business consultant David Baker says one of the most common mistakes a service firm can make is not having a defined, proprietary process. Writing in his subscription newsletter *Persuading* (available through his website, davidcbaker.com), Baker highlighted several reasons why a memorable methodology is important.

"Process is differentiating, highlighting the uniqueness of your firm with a process that you own," says Baker. Other advantages he cites are that a process demonstrates your experience, makes your work less accidental and will even allow you to charge more. "Clients are always willing to pay more for packages than individual hours within a fee structure."

A great memorable methodology, however, is never a cookie-cutter industry standard lifted from a textbook. Instead, it codifies a firm's particular method of problem-solving, typically identifying and sequencing multiple steps that often take place in the same, defined order. The process name should be trademarked to show that you value this piece of intellectual property.

Creating your memorable methodology is a great place to start to become a trusted authority who attracts high-paying clients.

A Little Rainmaker Arithmetic Might Change Your Mind

Do you think rainmaking is an expense or an investment? Your answer can have huge ramifications for attracting high-paying clients.

Many people, including your competitors, try to spend as little as possible on their marketing because they view it as an expense.

But a little arithmetic might change your mind.

"When you shift your mindset to seeing it as an investment you open up a new world of possibilities," says Michael Zipursky.

Zipursky is the CEO of Consulting Success and author of the book *ACT NOW*.[2] He has advised organizations like *Financial Times*, Dow Jones, RBC, and helped Panasonic launch new products into global markets, but more importantly, he's helped over 450 consultants from around the world in more than seventy-five industries add six and seven figures to their annual revenues.

"You can invest into more and better marketing, find new ways to create and deliver value for your ideal clients, and create an experience that they want to be part of," says Zipursky. "In a study we did, we found that people who invest more into their marketing have higher revenue and incomes than those that spend less on marketing."

Does the thought of spending thousands of dollars on marketing excite you?

"If you're like most business owners, you shudder at the thought of spending anything on marketing," says Zipursky. "However, this mindset is holding you back from attracting high-value clients, creating an advantage over your competition—and ultimately, winning more business."

The problem is that you are treating marketing as an expense instead of an investment.

"The best way to change your mindset is to understand your Customer Lifetime Value (CLV)," says Zipursky.

Here's a three-step exercise to figure out your CLV:

Step one. Calculate how much a client spends with you on an average engagement/project. Example: Your clients pay you $5,000 on a monthly retainer.

Step two. Determine how long your clients typically work with you. Example: You typically work with clients for eighteen months.

Step three. Multiply your average engagement value by the amount of time you work with your client. Example: $5,000 x 18 = $90,000.

Over their lifetime, clients like this are worth $90,000 to your business. That is your CLV.

If you do not charge a monthly fee, then use the average price of your project. Then, multiply it by how many times the client invests that amount to work with you over a twenty-four-month period, or longer if they typically stay longer.

The next calculation is to determine how much you are currently spending on marketing or business development. Be honest, do not include those expenses you hide in marketing like client entertainment and tickets to sporting events.

Marketing is what you do to get the attention and interest of your ideal clients so they want to have a conversation with you.

"If you know that your CLV is $90,000, how much are you open to investing to attract and win a new client?" asks Zipursky. The key word here is "invest." Stop looking at your marketing as an expense.

How much are you currently putting toward your marketing? Knowing your CLV puts into perspective how much you can invest in your marketing.

Most people hesitate to spend on marketing. But when you are clear on your CLV you'll not only feel more confident, but excited to invest 5 percent, 10 percent, even 15 percent or more into building a robust pipeline of qualified prospects.

MAKE IT RAIN

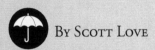 By Scott Love

Here is how to win the great rainmaking gamble. Several years ago, I learned how to count cards and worked as a professional card-counting blackjack player. I taught myself how to play by reading books. I got good at counting and wanted to take my game to a whole new level.

The MIT Blackjack Team is the very same team that earned notoriety in Ben Maizrich's book *Bringing Down the House*,[3] later turned into the motion picture *Twenty-One*. I did some research on the players of the team and found that two of the former members were involved in business, so I reached out to them and introduced myself and offered to advise them on sales strategy as a consultant in exchange for being mentored by them on card counting.

We met several times in person and they helped me increase my skill to a point that I was a highly effective card counter. This went on for nearly two years and ended when I lost interest in the game and instead started playing poker. Poker is a more interesting game because of the people element of it. With blackjack, the whole game is based on math. There is an inherent defect in the game that gives a player who knows how to detect it through counting cards a tangible advantage over the house. There is nothing wrong or immoral or illegal with counting cards, if you are just using your brain and not any mechanical or electrical device.

In counting cards, the essence of the game is based on probability. This is a very simple concept: Put money on the felt when you have an advantage, and don't put money on the felt when you do not. As in business, one needs to expend and exert energy in proportion to the likelihood of a favorable outcome.

Read the above paragraph again, but this time start the paragraph with "In the business of developing new business." Expend your time and energy in areas where you have a high likelihood of a favorable outcome. And if your primary objective is not realized, structure your energy in a way that you still have something to show for your efforts.

How does this apply to client development?

There are only five avenues of getting new business. That is it. Just five.

Here they are in the order that they are ranked. The top of the list has the highest likelihood of a favorable outcome. The bottom of the list has the least likely way of bearing fruit.

Let me elaborate on each avenue.

Existing clients. This is obviously at the top of the list. If you need new business, seek those who have given you business before. They have seen first-hand that you have delivered value.

Those who know you. These are people whom you have met at trade conferences but did not buy from you. They are people you pitched business to, but you were not awarded the contract. There is a relationship, yet it did not end up in the transference of money or value. But they know you.

Referrals. When you are referred to someone else, you are borrowing their trust and that borrowed trust helps you open doors.

People who have heard of you. They saw you give a presentation at a conference but did not meet you. They read an article you wrote. They heard others mention your name.

Cold contacts. These are people who have not bought from you, do not know you, have no common connections with you (or none that are realized), and have never heard of you. They are completely cold, and therefore they are at the bottom of the list. They have the least likely probability of bearing fruit. *Yet this is the area in which many professionals spend most of their energy pursuing.*

Please read that last line again. Do not spend time in areas that have a low likelihood of a favorable outcome. This is gambling and is the same reason why casinos are so profitable. It is because those playing their games are predicted to lose over time because they are betting when they have an unfavorable advantage.

PART II

HOW RAINMAKING EXPERTS MAKE IT RAIN

SECRET #3

Identify Client Motivations To Hire You

The frustrated sales rep became annoyed with Sam (true story, name changed to protect confidentiality) when he told her that he really did not see any reason to buy her product. She tried close #17 on him, right after rebuttal #34.

"Would you like for me to just give you some money?" Sam asked her.

She seemed puzzled and asked what Sam meant. "I feel like you do not care about how your product can benefit me personally, because you haven't shown me that. I am getting the feeling that all you really want is your commission and that your heart isn't committed to benefitting me through your product."

She left the office frustrated and confused because she did not get the sale. Sam went back to work puzzled why a sales manager would spend so much time training a sales rep on the tactics of the sale but neglect the key component to effective sales relationships: knowledge of the personal benefits of the product or service, and how to effectively communicate those personal benefits.

Forget about sales tactics. Instead, focus on buying motives. If you are selling your product or service to your customer, and you have nothing else in mind but to serve your prospect, then this will come through to them and make the sale much easier to close. This concept is from Jeffrey Gitomer, a successful sales trainer in Charlotte, North Carolina, and author of books such as *Little Red Book of Selling*.[4]

In the world of professional services business development, this is a critical component to convey your value to your prospective client. For a key executive in a company to select the services of a law firm or an accounting firm or other professional service, this is incredibly important.

People hate to have the feeling that they are being sold something. But the typical sales professional keeps using sales trick #19 that was first developed in 1972, hoping to close their prospect without any regard for the potential benefit to the end user. What worked in the past in rainmaking will not work today.

Consider this concept: Forget about features and benefits. Nobody really cares about the features and benefits of your products and services. Instead, they care about their own personal benefits that are derived from your product or service. People only make decisions that personally benefit them, so that is what you need to target with your prospect. If you are involved in client development, you can develop authentic and meaningful relationships with your prospects when you think this way.

MAKE IT RAIN

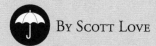 By Scott Love

Here are three ways to develop a solid business development plan based on the buying motives of those you wish to reach:

Consider your own offering. Find out why the past ten clients or customers bought from you. The reasons you think they purchased it might be totally different from their real reasons, so you need to find out what they are. Think of those clients who are very dependent upon you and where there is something of a personal relationship. For those where this makes sense, call them, and ask them to tell you the main problem they had that made them choose to buy from you before. This will give you a baseline of information. You might think they chose you because of the brand equity of your law firm, but I'd be willing to bet that there was a specific problem that needed to be solved. If you drill down enough, you'll find that perhaps there was a personal motivation to buy from you, something driven by the personal self-interests of your client rather than from the perspective of only what was in the interests of the organization.

Ask your prospect why he or she would buy it before you even go into your presentation. Ask this question before you even present your product or service: "What criteria is important to you in the purchase of services similar to ours?" Find out *exactly* what is important to them, simply by asking them. You now have a buying motive. Sell to that motive, not to what you think it might be. If you do enough research, you'll notice that there are specific trends, and you might discover some reasons why your clients prefer you over your competitors. Pay attention to this.

With your colleagues, determine what the personal benefits of your service are by drilling down with these questions: If you work in a professional services firm or organization where there are many people involved in client development, I'd highly recommend having meetings to discuss the details of client activities. As you all are tied together in your organization, you can be more transparent about specific clients and matters. In a meeting with them, discuss as a group why your clients have bought from you. Perhaps share the ideas in this chapter with them and then revert to discussing point by point why your clients selected you and your firm over your competition.

You may find trends and data that can serve as key drivers for future client development efforts. You can follow this exercise and logically peel back the onion skin of motivations to get to the heart of why your clients bought from you. You can follow this logic in your analysis: First, what are the features of my service? Second, what are the benefits? Third, what are the benefits of those benefits? This pulls the onion skin back and lets you consider more of an intrinsic motivation that already exists in the motives of your clients and prospects. And fourth, how and why would a prospect benefit from this service or product on a personal level?

What would those personal benefits be? When would they be realized? This last series of questions gets to the heart of why people buy. I'm sure that you will enjoy sharing stories of how clients benefited personally from working with you. This is where client loyalty begins, when people see that their own personal livelihood is dependent upon a professional service provider.

The discoveries from this process will give you key information that can be utilized as a proactive way to communicate your value during client development meetings and calls. These minor changes are truly the essence of major achievement, and you'll find this authentic way to sell your services will attract more prospects.

Avoid The Biggest Rainmaking Mistake

Are you flushing marketing dollars down the toilet? The biggest mistake in small business marketing is forgetting the phrase "lifetime value of a client." Understanding this strategy can leave your cheaper competition in the dust.

Most small business owners see ad and marketing spends as a make-it-or-break-it-the-first-time proposition. That is a big miscalculation.

"If this were dating it would be like asking for marriage on the first date," says author Jim Kaspari. "We're throwing thousands of dollars down the toilet with this mistake."

The goal of ads and marketing used to be to get paying clients and to make sales right away. That makes perfect sense, but it simply doesn't work anymore. Marketers need to be thinking about the long-term.

"Many of us are using our marketing time, energy, creativity, and brilliant brains doing pay-per-click online advertising and trying to get over 100 percent return on investment with the first transaction," says Kaspari. "That's just crazy."

Kaspari is a long-term thinker. He worked at Genentech, Inc. for twenty years as a chemical engineer, automation and systems analyst, and training manager. By investing well and helping start businesses as a moonlighting side hustle while working, he was able to retire a millionaire at the age of forty-four.

"We all know that much of marketing has gone online, but why is it so challenging and time-consuming these days and what can you do about it?" asks Kaspari.

That is a driving question for Kaspari when he works with clients. Kaspari has been a business coach and consultant with entrepreneurial business owners and start-ups since 2005 and has coached more than five hundred clients in nine countries.

Kaspari, CEO of PEAK Business Coaching, is the author of *PEAK Profits*.[5] He has spoken on stages across the United States and in Australia on small business marketing.

Kaspari advises his audiences to think about and quickly calculate the lifetime valuation of your average client.

"Don't get hung up on the details," says Kaspari. "For example, a hairstylist might have an average client spend of $75 per day, they come in every month, and this lasts two years. That comes out to $1,800."

This knowledge can lead to different behavior. "Instead of maxing out at $5 per lead (20 percent conversion, 300 percent ROI to cover other costs), you can easily spend $10–$15 per lead or more and make out like a bandit," says Kaspari. "This strategy leaves your cheaper competition in the dust."

The other key is realizing that we aren't looking for a sale with our ads. People don't want to be sold to anymore. So, what's our new goal? To make friends. Get to know each other—draw them in with an irresistible gift and then help them solve problems and make their life better. This allows them to get to know, like, and trust us.

"Interview your clients until you know what is irresistible to them," says Kaspari. "Create an opt-in for your website or lead page. Set up an autoresponder email series that gives tremendous, relevant value, help, and great ideas and resources. After five to seven of these emails, you're safe to ask if you can be of further help to them (sell something). Then it's lather, rinse, and repeat."

Is Networking Over? No, But It Is Morphing

When we ranked the top ways to attract high-paying clients in our rainmaker confidential research studies, networking always finished in the top four. Networking on Zoom may be an answer.

Yes, the Zoom fatigue struggle is real. But let's look at some important issues:

What can a busy professional do to incorporate attracting high-paying clients into their current workday? What can you do virtually? When we get back to networking with real, live people and not a Zoom room, what are the best strategies? How can you build relationships in the new normal?

The question was posed to Dena Lefkowitz, a former lawyer with a national practice developing marketing strategies for attorneys.

Lefkowitz has two suggestions: "First, adapt the mindset that getting work is as important as doing work and you've got to find time. Priorities may need adjusting. Second, make your extracurricular activities a blend of personally intriguing and professionally rewarding."

MAKE IT RAIN

 Asked for some specific extracurricular activities, Lefkowitz was ready with a list:

Use passion. "Pick something you're interested in so there will be a good chance of follow-through. An area of passion helps you stay engaged."

Make it a target-rich environment. "Make sure there is a likelihood that your ideal clients or referral sources (someone who serves your ideal client in a different capacity) are involved with that organization or activity."

Vet the group first. "Once you've targeted an activity or organization, vet it to make sure your valuable networking time is spent wisely."

Check the schedule. "Look ahead and pick events. Register and put them on your calendar. Connect in advance with others who are attending or identify who you want to meet. Create these anchors that make it harder to blow off networking."

Ask and listen. "Think ahead about how to present yourself. Who are you? What problem do you solve? Whom do you serve? These are good ingredients of an initial introduction. Have some ice-breaker questions to ask and listen carefully to what you hear. That's the gold you'll mine later."

Lefkowitz emphasizes the importance of making going to market a professionally satisfying activity; otherwise, you'll dread and avoid it. "You must go to market," she stresses, "so why not make it more fun by finding things you really care about and doing them with people you like, who you can help, and vice versa? You can make time for that, even when you're busy."

"If you hire me to be your new sales rep, you'll get a
complete money-back guarantee! And if you act now,
you'll also receive a set of Amazing Ginsu Knives –
a $99 value – absolutely free! But wait, there's more!"

SECRET #4

Hone Your Personal Rainmaking Brand

Perhaps you have heard this joke: If you kill someone, the best place to hide the body is on the second page of the search results on Google.

If you want to attract high-paying clients, it pays to improve your Google search rankings. This is important because in a rare moment of transparency, Google officials revealed details in October 2019 of its top-secret search algorithm. The tech execs say changes are being rolled out that will surface more accurate and intelligent responses to hundreds of millions of queries each day.

Some of those queries will involve you.

Google briefed the media on its "Bidirectional Encoder Representations from Transformers" (or "Bert" to its friends) as being among the largest improvements to search in half a decade.

You do not need to understand how Google has harnessed mathematical modeling and machine learning for complex searches. This is not about how to game the algorithm or buy specific key ad words.

Oh, and Google announced the new search algorithm would be used as part of its $136 billion advertising business. Obviously.

What might not be so obvious is the importance of Google to your credibility.

A woman came to a speech and approached the speaker to say that before she decided to come, she had Googled him. "That's funny," he replied, "I had a strange sense that I was being Googled."

Face facts, prospects are Googling you.

For attracting high-paying clients, Google is more important as part of your lead conversion process than your lead generation process. Here's what we mean. Lead generation is how expert consultants and professionals attract prospects. Lead conversion is how experts convince prospects to hire them, and it is important at this stage to demonstrate credibility.

Here is how to demonstrate credibility by increasing your search rankings: do more activities that get on Google.

The publisher for one of the books by coauthor Henry DeVries said by the date his book launched Henry should be working to fill five pages of Google with search results about his book and his work. The publisher said people judge him by the amount of Google hits there are. This makes sense.

In California they say the universe rewards activity. In the Midwest they say the Lord helps those who help themselves (the authors of this book are bilingual). To get more Google hits you need to help yourself by doing more things that get posted on Google.

If you are an expert who wants to attract more high-paying clients, do the following to increase your credibility:

1. Post articles on your LinkedIn page and pay attention to the article topics.

2. Write a book and make sure it is listed for sale on various bookselling websites.

3. Create an audio version of your book that sells on Audible.

4. Get booked to give speeches that get promoted by the sponsors online.

5. Post how-to videos about your expertise on YouTube.

6. Distribute tips news releases on Cision PR Newswire.

7. Become a columnist for a respected news outlet.

8. Get booked to speak on podcasts that are promoted online.

Just as Google is working to fine-tune its search engine, you should be working to improve your search results.

How To Reinvigorate Your Personal Brand

Does eating at McDonald's make me look fat? Does drinking Pabst Blue Ribbon beer make me look frat? Does shipping with UPS make me look flat?

Does your personal brand suffer from a brand identity crisis? That can stop an independent professional or small service firm dead in its tracks from attracting high-paying clients. Typically, the problem is messaging that is off.

So, change the messaging and change the narrative. McDonald's now sells salads. Pabst isn't just for frat parties; it now has a hot global reputation. UPS now makes brown logistics look cool.

Face it, you already have a brand, but is it the brand you want? A brand is what clients and prospects perceive about you. Some call it the brand promise. You need to make sure your brand promise messaging says what you want to communicate. A brand identity is too important to leave to chance or fix down the road.

How can a messaging mismatch cause you a brand identity crisis?

In an interview Christine Alemany, CEO at TBGA, shared her views:

"A common problem for marketers is learning that the brand identity isn't resonating with its intended customers," says Alemany.

Alemany is a trusted expert in reinvigorating brands. She advises start-ups through Columbia Business School's Entrepreneurial Sounding Board and is a teaching fellow at the NASDAQ Entrepreneurial Center.

"What I find a lot is the internal confusion or frustration, especially as companies grow," says Alemany. "If the founders aren't 100 percent aligned as they grow, what typically happens is the silos start moving in different directions."

The bottom line: As your team grows, make sure everyone on the team is communicating the right brand promise.

MAKE IT RAIN

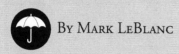 By Mark LeBlanc

The easiest way to position yourself by concept is to create a great Defining Statement. A Defining Statement is a simple answer to a simple question, "What do you do?"

When you can answer this simple question in a succinct and concise way, you will have reached a deeper level of attraction or connection with your prospects. In time and with conviction you might find yourself with more prospects than you can handle.

It is not easy. In fact, it may be one of the hardest assignments you will undertake in your business. The rewards can be great. While there are several reasons you will benefit from having a Defining Statement; here is one of the better reasons:

You will command better pricing or higher fees.

It's true. Whatever you charge for what you sell is more likely to be perceived as an investment in the outcomes you provide versus a cost for satisfying a need or solving a problem.

How many times do you answer this question differently? Do your prospects, clients, or even your family and friends really understand what you do? What if everyone knew, understood, or better yet, could repeat your Defining Statement? You would take your business to the next level. Now, that would make the hard work worth it.

Make Sure Your Personal Brand Doesn't Suck On Zoom

Patrick McGowan has some hard news for you: people are judging you on Zoom.

"Amateur hour is over," says McGowan, founder of Punch'n, a video presence company. "The days of looking like a Dateline interview of someone from the Witness Protection Program need to be behind us."

Having to live your work life on Zoom is hard. The most popular quote of 2020 will be, "You are on mute." And worse than that is making comments when you don't realize you are not muted. As Seth Rogen tweeted, "I call my Zoom meeting look 'laced up from the waist up.'"

Another favorite tweet, from Snarky Mommy, is: "There's awkward and then there's 'the Zoom meeting is over, and you and one other person can't figure out how to leave the meeting' awkward."

This is no news flash: "Zoom is the top brand that people have increased usage of during the pandemic," according to MBLM's *Brand Intimacy COVID Study*,[6] a study of brands based on emotions during the pandemic. Purell and Netflix follow Zoom and rank second and third, respectively, for increased usage during COVID.

"We need to approach our video meetings with the same level of care and intentionality as we do our in-person meetings," says McGowan, who works with people who want to level up their video presence. "How we show up defines us and defines our personal brand."

McGowan reminds us of the adage that a picture is worth a thousand words. "But a video is worth ten thousand words. At thirty frames per second, the camera doesn't lie."

Zoom fatigue can be remedied with a strong purpose. "When we are intentional about bringing our best self to our video events, our authentic self and our value gets communicated and we make a positive impression."

MAKE IT RAIN

 Here are four tips from McGowan on how to improve your personal brand through Zoom:

Show up five minutes early. "Every pilot goes through a flight check to make sure *all systems are go*. We should do the same thing if we want to make a positive impression. I often launch a 'new appointment' on Zoom to check that I have the right camera, microphone, and speaker selected. I'll exit that meeting on Zoom and then log in to the scheduled appointment. Additionally, we can all schedule meetings for forty-five minutes rather than sixty minutes. Different times get different rules."

Frame thyself. "We want to use the *rule of thirds* to position ourselves a little off-center. Shifting to the left or right of center and having your eyes at about a third of the way down from the top positions you in a photographically ideal position. This shows you are intentional about how you appear on camera and subtly communicates that you are someone to watch. To achieve this, folks often stack a small pile of books (cookbooks work well) and place the camera at about eyebrow-level and then angle it slightly downward about five to ten degrees. I recommend starting with a webcam, rather than a laptop camera, and to put it on a small, desktop tripod that allows you to tilt the camera."

Comfort = Confidence. "When I first began to use Zoom on a regular basis, I used either my laptop camera or a webcam. I didn't feel like I could sit naturally or comfortably for either. Through this I discovered how much I contorted my body, shoulders, and neck to fit into view of the camera. This is one reason why I recommend starting with a webcam rather than a laptop camera and to put it on a small desktop tripod with the ability to tilt the camera. Framing yourself sitting comfortably gives your team, audience, and viewers a sense of calm. It also begins to define your video presence."

Let them see your eyes. "While we are biologically drawn to look at people's faces when we can, on video calls it's vital we let our viewers see our eyes. This means we must become comfortable looking at the camera instead of our monitor. This takes practice and time to develop our own personal style of presenting over video. Remember, at thirty frames per second, the camera doesn't lie. When people can see our eyes, we are more approachable and watchable."

A bonus tip from McGowan is to focus on viewers. He says this is actually pretty easy: 1) Shut off self-view; then 2) Stop thinking about what you look like or sound like on video.

"We want to shift our focus to why we are in this meeting or virtual event," says McGowan. "For most of us we have something to give that is of value to another human being. We want to ultimately connect with someone. It's near impossible to focus on other people when we're looking at ourselves in the mirror."

Why Your LinkedIn Is Not Attracting High-Paying Clients

If you want to use LinkedIn to attract high-paying clients, don't talk about how you are going to help. Be the rare consultant or professional on the platform who just starts helping.

That's the advice of the person who is arguably America's top LinkedIn thought leader, Ellen Melko Moore. She has consulted with the Oprah Winfrey Book Club, the Zappos guys, and now teaches LinkedIn social selling strategies for some of the top thought leaders in the digital marketing space. She is the LinkedIn trainer of the year for the American Marketing Association.

"If you're looking to connect with ambitious, successful, high-fee B2B clients, LinkedIn is the place you will find them," says Moore. "For the most part, they are not hanging out on Facebook or Instagram looking for real solutions to their business problems."

As for those important leaders who weren't using LinkedIn much prior to the quarantine adventures of 2020, they're active now.

"Anyone can make themselves look expert on other platforms, but only LinkedIn lets you see the whole history of that person's actual work," says Moore. "You can draw your own conclusions."

MAKE IT RAIN

 Here are four ways from Moore to up your LinkedIn game:

Slow down, focus on quality over quantity. Social media trends of the last decade have most experts convinced that digital marketing and sales are always about the numbers, but LinkedIn often works much better if professionals and consultants treat their LinkedIn network as a highly valuable asset. "In other words, slow down, go steady, and focus on the quality of your network rather than the quantity," says Moore. "Work on developing deeper relationships with the people who are best suited to be desirable clients or best placed to be powerful referral partners. We have one thought leader client who has 150 connections, but every single one of those people has real influence. He is killing it."

Redo your personal LinkedIn profile and make it for your target audience. "Instead of making your personal LinkedIn profile about you, or about your company, make it *for* your most important target audience, client, or partner," says Moore. "Think of your profile in a content marketing context versus a promotional or historical context. Most professionals on LinkedIn—when they are ready to buy—are going to buy from the first person who gives them a significant shift in insight. So, don't waste your LinkedIn profile—especially the 'About' section— talking about yourself or your company. Instead, focus on dropping those value bombs—so visitors to your profile can learn something that's important to *them*.

Stay away from automation and go easy on templates. Many professionals want a "Done For Me" strategy on LinkedIn, which has given rise to multiple LinkedIn lead generation companies that will help leaders craft templated messages and then use automation to send those messages, inviting hundreds of professionals a day to connect and communicate with that leader. "The only problem is that LinkedIn is cracking down on these companies and using automation can get you kicked off the platform," says Moore. "LinkedIn really wants to emphasize their platform as a network, not a place to 'buy leads' on social media. Consider adopting this strategy instead: each day, find two to five high-quality people with whom you'd like to connect. Send a connection request that is personal and specific versus something that could be sent to thousands of people who resemble this person."

LinkedIn is a mystery to almost everyone on the platform. The pandemic has boosted LinkedIn's popularity, with 660 million users at the start of 2021. "More importantly, 55 percent of decision makers use LinkedIn content to choose the organizations with whom they want to work," says Moore. "And one in five investors say it's the best place to learn about a topic. But despite LinkedIn's growing popularity, it's hard to find people who express confidence in using the platform for professional or business development. Many thought leaders who are powerful and popular in other mediums aren't sure how to handle LinkedIn."

The bottom line: All this is good news for those who choose to optimize LinkedIn. It means you have a real chance of making progress quickly if you put in some attention, intention, and practice offering help, not hype.

Kill That Old Elevator Speech

Most business development elevator speeches do not reach the top floor: the decision maker's brain.

Let's say you are successful at getting a conversation (probably virtual) with a decision maker. Or you bump into a decision maker through networking (maybe virtual too). How do you answer their question, "What do you do?"

"Do not begin by talking about yourself," says Bryan Gray, CEO of Revenue Path Group. "Instead, open with something powerful that will create value. The first thirty-to-forty-five seconds are crucial."

Gray advises beginning your first few precious seconds discussing their pains. Then tell a story about them because that involves them emotionally. Discoveries in neuroscience prove decision-making is largely emotional, not logical. So how can you persuade the emotional part of the brain?

"Do not get the order wrong because this is a contest to win over the primitive brain," says Gray. "If you start with a story, you will lose the brain."

From there you are going to engage in a conversation. A brain that is conversing about how to solve its pains is a fully engaged brain.

"The day I realized I was selling to a three-pound organ called the brain, my life changed," said Gray. "When I discovered there's a pathway to decision-making, I felt I could make the adjustment.

MAKE IT RAIN

 Once when bestselling author and speaker Judy Carter was on a plane, a C-level executive sitting next to her asked the question: "What do you do?"

The way she answered the question made Carter $160,000.

"So how did I answer that question? First, I started by asking her to tell me a little about what she did and her business."

The executive talked about all the stress she deals with while working in HR and dealing with nonmilitary contractors. "The mood in the department is just dismal, we can't keep up with demands, and the government is constantly changing things on us. People are working long hours, and everybody is cranky," she said.

Then Carter gave her elevator pitch that addressed the pain:

"All right, let me tell you what I do," said Carter, author of the book *The Message of You.*[7] "You know how change and all the new government policies like you are dealing with and downsizing creates all this frustration? Well, I spent years as a headlining stand-up comic, and I wrote a book that was on *Oprah* about how to turn problems into punchlines (*The Comedy Bible*[8]) and I speak on stress reduction. I use a very unusual technique. I speak on the techniques of comedy, using something as simple as your sense of humor to solve problems.

"And believe me, I know about problems, especially from growing up with an alcoholic father. So what I do is show people how to use comedy and improv as a communications and stress reduction tool. I show people how not to leave their sense of humor at home, but how to use it appropriately at work and even use it as a speaking and leadership tool. What are the results I get? Well, my clients tell me after I speak, they hear laughter at work. Let's face it, Corporate America has become humor-impaired. People need laughter and that laughter has great results as conflict turns into camaraderie when people communicate better. One client said that after I spoke people were saying: 'Thank God it's Monday.'"

This total stranger on the plane said to Carter, "Oh my God, do we need you."

"She hired me fifteen minutes into the flight," said Carter. "And that turned into speaking gigs for many areas of the military: the Air Force, the Army, and spouse groups. I got so many referrals, all from that one stranger on a plane asking me, 'What do you do?'"

That is the rainmaking power of an elevator pitch that reaches the brain of a decision maker.

SECRET #5

Write Your Next Book Fast

The best time for a rainmaker is not when they publish their first book but their second. That way, when someone says they would like to read your book, you can nonchalantly reply: "Oh, which one?"

There has never been a better time to write the right book. Look to prolific authors for inspiration on how to do it quickly.

Ian Fleming, the author of the James Bond novels, famously preferred to do his writing every morning in the sunroom of his Caribbean island beach house, pausing just once at lunch to enjoy a glass of rum, a swim in the ocean, and a nice nap before returning to the task.

That's all well and good for a spy-thriller novelist, but for those of us without the private beach, a more thoughtful and efficient approach to book writing is necessary. Writing an entire book is a long-term project, and, like all long-term projects, putting in smart groundwork will save you time and keep your momentum going.

When it comes to writing great business books fast, look to bestselling author and award-winning public speaker Dianna Booher. Booher is the Stephen King of the consultant book. With forty-eight books to her name, the prolific Booher is something of an expert on staying productive for the long haul. Her books are translated into sixty-two foreign language editions, with nearly four million copies in print. Her publishers include Simon & Schuster, HarperCollins, Penguin Random House, McGraw-Hill, and Berrett-Koehler.

MAKE IT RAIN

 Here are Booher's tips for how she approaches writing a book:

Outline your content—forget the seat-of-the-pants approach used by some novelists. "'Pantsers,' as these novelists call themselves, write from scene to scene wherever the story and characters take them. That may be a fine approach for novelists, but not for those writing nonfiction. Just as people start with a blueprint to build a house, writing in the most productive way calls for a plan."

Research first—not "as you go" chapter by chapter. "You'd never consider building a house room by room— kitchen first, then bathrooms, then maybe the bedrooms next. Instead, you organize the project by tasks: the foundation, then the framing, then the plumbing, then the electrical, and so forth. It's the same with book writing. Researching chapter by chapter is counterproductive. You'll soon discover you're chasing down duplicate information. Additionally, most authors are also readers, which means once they dig into a trove of survey responses, academic studies, or humorous opinion pieces, they get hooked.

They leap from one article or study to the next, forgetting their ultimate writing goal, to collect ideas and statistics to support their book. Don't let yourself go down that road. Instead, grab all the information you need in a focused research effort, and then go back to writing."

Conduct a writing marathon. "Separate yourself physically and mentally from the routine. Lock yourself away in your home office. Some author friends check into a hotel. Do whatever works for you to stay focused for about twelve straight hours for seven to ten consecutive days. Do the necessary things during the day (like getting dressed, eating, exercising) as your stretch breaks from writing."

Never reread as you draft. "Stopping to reread will stall your momentum. Rereading to edit is a totally separate step that comes after drafting."

Check email only once daily just after you stop writing for the day. "You'll be too tired to write long emails, so answer the necessary ones briefly and hit send. Those critical messages will be waiting for the recipient the next morning when they begin work."

Stay off social media. "Schedule your posts ahead of your marathon or have an assistant to post them for you. You may even post a note that you'll be 'on sabbatical writing' for X days and sign off completely."

Keep a daily log of output. "Record the date and how many pages and words you write each day. Then keep a running total as you sprint to the finish line. Seeing that

> total word count grow, you'll build momentum, and find
> yourself writing faster and faster to 'the end.'"

Why You Should Coauthor A Business Book

Ken Blanchard, a man who has sold millions and millions of business books, once told coauthor Henry DeVries in an interview: "You know, I have never authored a business book."

"Ken, are you pulling my leg?" Henry asked. "You've authored more than fifty business books."

"No, I have *coauthored* fifty business books," said Blanchard. "I know what I know; I want to know what other people know too."

Blanchard's impact as a thought leader is far reaching. *The One Minute Manager*—the iconic 1982 classic that he coauthored with the late Spencer Johnson—sold more than thirteen million copies and in 2015 was revised and released as *The New One Minute Manager*.[9]

Blanchard has now coauthored sixty-five books whose combined sales total more than twenty-eight million copies. His groundbreaking works—including *Raving Fans, The Secret,* and *Leading at a Higher Level,* to name just a few—have been translated into forty-seven languages. In 2005 Ken was inducted into Amazon's Hall of Fame as one of the top twenty-five bestselling authors of all time.

In June 2020 Blanchard and bestselling author Gibson Sylvestre released a recorded conversation (audiobook) aimed at promoting unity and racial diversity. Having lived eighty-one years, Blanchard, a close friend, and mentor to Sylvestre, explained how his mother taught him to love and accept people from all backgrounds regardless of color or creed. More than five decades separate Blanchard and Sylvestre in terms of age; however, their love for God, family, country, servant leadership, corporate training, business, and sports united them in a dynamic way. "My mother taught me that God doesn't make junk," said Blanchard.

MAKE IT RAIN

 By Henry DeVries

In January 2021, the world lost a great author, Diane Gage Lofgren. Or should I say a great coauthor. She taught me how to be a coauthor back in 1991 when we cowrote my first book, *Self-Marketing Secrets*.[10] Lofgren taught others to be a great coauthor too. To quote from her obituary written by Roger Bolton:

"Although an extraordinarily successful CCO and CMO, she also was the author of nine books and scores of magazine articles on personal and business relationships. One of her most popular books, with coauthor Margaret Bhola, was *Women I Want to Grow Old With*, a book designed to help women be intentional about making and sustaining female friendships. The authors were passionate about encouraging women to learn from each other and to strengthen their safety net of female friends.[11]

Here are some important lessons Lofgren taught about being a coauthor:

Decide who will be listed as the lead author. The author who has the most claim to the content of the book is the lead author. Gage was the second author on my book. I was the second author on a book I coauthored with Tom Searcy, because the idea was his. Blanchard is often the second author listed on many of his books. It is not determined by who is most famous or has the biggest platform.

Decide if the book ownership will be 50/50 or 51/49. Some of my books are 50/50 percent and some are 51/49 percent. One bestselling author I know will only do 51/49 deals because he was burned on a 50/50 deal after he had a falling out with his coauthor. She then blocked him from using the book topic as a speech topic.

Decide what the split of royalties will be. This can be 50/50 or some other split. I have even heard of a 95/5 deal. Everything in life is a negotiation.

Decide how you will approach the writing. One way is to split the chapters and have each writer do half the chapters and then trade for editing. Another strategy is to have one author write the first drafts and the other author write the polished chapters. There are many right answers, but the approach must be decided upon in advance and agreed upon as equitable. I have coauthored ten books and each approach was different.

Decide how you will approach the editing and proofing. Any book worth writing is worth writing a first draft that is sucky. The real magic happens in the editing. Proofing is the last step, and the coauthors are not best suited to this because they are too close.

Decide how you will market the book. Books don't market authors; authors market books. The number one way to promote a book is to talk about it in speeches, podcasts, and radio and TV interviews. More people are affected by hearing about the book than by reading the book.

Decide how you will split paid speaking engagements because of the book. An expert with a bestselling business book speaks in the $5,000 to $10,000 range. Coauthors should decide how to split offers to speak when they come in out of the blue. The truth is coauthors must market themselves to gain speaking opportunities, following the "You Eat What You Hunt" philosophy.

The bottom line: Two minds are better than one when it comes to a great business book. Great business books share the why, the how, and the what's next for readers. The readers supply the when. Overall, the coauthors must create a book they love, because if they don't love the book, how can they get others to love it?

Top Ten Ways To Use Social Media To Make Your Book A Bestseller

Books don't promote rainmaker authors; rainmaker authors promote books. An author who writes a book to promote their business needs to shine the spotlight on the book in hopes of gaining buzz.

When it comes to promotion, Minal Sampat is an immigrant who thinks big. In 2013, at the age of twenty-eight, she launched her first marketing company by breaking a Guinness World Record.

Born in India, Sampat grew up in St. Thomas, US Virgin Islands, and now resides in the state of Washington with her husband. In 2020 Sampat used her social media skills to make her book, *Why Your Marketing is Killing Your Business & What to do About It*,[12] an international Amazon bestseller.

The dirty little secret of books is that unless you are a celebrity, the publisher expects the author to promote the book. Even if you are a celebrity, the publisher expects the author to do most of the promotion. Naturally, the best place to promote is to go direct to readers with social media.

MAKE IT RAIN

 Here are Sampat's top ten ways to use social media to create a bestseller:

Start marketing with an intention. "Even if you are trying to simply do brand awareness about the book," says Sampat.

Understand how algorithms work. Learn how the social media algorithms such as Facebook and Instagram work and plan your strategy around it. The more you know, the better your marketing plan will be. "Whatever platform you are most active on, learn the algorithm for that platform," she says.

Build your audience in advance. Leverage the organic reach by building an audience that would be genuinely interested in your book and topic. Sampat focused on people in business who are readers and liked content about books.

More of them, less you. Make your marketing message about *them*, and not *you* by highlighting the readers and spotlighting them in your marketing. "It's about them, it's not about you, is the attitude to have," says Sampat.

Offer downloads. Share content that is attached with the book, but can be easily downloaded such as worksheets, graphs, and checklists.

Continuously show appreciation for the readers and the book. When you focus on connecting and not promotion, you will continue to do better with your marketing. Sampat always highlighted readers on Facebook and Instagram. She created dialogue with readers and shared news about their business. "Nobody expected that from a random book they bought," said Sampat.

Share, share, share. On a weekly basis, share digestible content from the books such as quotes, lines, and chapter page photos.

Share your journey as an author. Readers want to connect with you. Give them a glimpse "behind the scenes."

Show off social proof. For example, share testimonials and reviews. Sampat would take screenshots from Amazon reviews to show what people thought of her book.

> **Always offer book copies at webinars, conferences, and seminars.** If you are teaching a course, use the book as required reading. And why not? Shouldn't students get your best thoughts?

In 2021 Sampat launched Marketologist, an online marketing strategy school for healthcare practitioners, coaches/consultants/speakers, and aspiring marketing ambassadors. To learn more or get in touch, please go to MinalSampat.com.

SECRET #6

Speak Up, But Only If You Want To Make It Rain

With a suspenseful and entertaining speech titled "An Unbelievable Story," Aaron Beverly, a thirty-year-old JP Morgan project manager from Philadelphia, won the Toastmasters World Championship of Public Speaking in August 2019.

"Aaron Beverly's speech was brilliant and had all the elements of a spy movie," said Ed Tate, a Certified Speaking Professional and the 2000 Toastmasters' World Champion of Public Speaking. "It included five setups and payoffs and had all of the elements: espionage, intrigue, danger, drama, and deception."

You can watch Beverly's winning speech on YouTube.

"My mother told me to be myself throughout my life and not change who I am in order to be liked and accepted by other people," said Beverly. "Only within recent years has this advice seeped into my speeches.

His winning speech was about acceptance despite differences and told the story of his humorous adventure as the only African American in attendance at his friend's wedding in India.

MAKE IT RAIN

 Beverly shared his advice for being a more impactful speaker:

Be your authentic self on stage. "Unfortunately, there is a notion among many speakers that you must have overly theatrical gestures, special props, and flowery language. The result, in most of these cases, is a performance that appears disingenuous, phony, or just plain awkward."

Know who your audience is. "It is the number one golden rule. If you don't know who your audience is, how they typically like their information, the type of words and language that they use, you set yourself up for failure before you even begin because if you don't know your audience, you can't connect with your audience."

Establish a connection. "One way you can do this is by sharing engaging, relatable personal stories. These can include stories about the workplace or even my favorite, family stories. A relatable story can create an emotional bond with your audience that then leads to establishing a connection."

Five Worst Mistakes To Make In Your Speech Opening

Are you polite when you start a speech? Well, cut it out.
Do you share learning objectives? Stop it. Right now.

Are you willing to share your personal story? Please do not do that.

We asked communications expert Neil Gordon to share the five biggest mistakes he feels most speakers make when starting a speech.

Gordon says the challenge is to razzle-dazzle the audience in the first seven seconds. And that is a tall order. He works with authors and helps them get six-figure book advances, be seen on shows like *Ellen* and *Dr. Oz*, and double their speaking fees. Gordon has ghostwritten or collaborated on books published by Penguin Random House, HarperCollins, and Hay House. So, he is kind of a big deal.

MAKE IT RAIN

 In Gordon's opinion, here are the five biggest opening mistakes public speakers make:

They Start With Politeness. "Your audience will develop an impression of you within the first fifteen seconds of your presentation. But saying things like 'Thank you for having me' squanders that impression. To milk the tension that starts your speech, take the stage after you've been introduced and, perhaps after a brief pause, go right into the first critical line of your speech."

They Begin With Their Learning Objectives. "Speakers falsely think it will help their audience absorb their material by laying out everything they'll be discussing at the beginning. But this would be like the creators of *Avengers Infinity War* laying out everything that's going to happen in *Endgame* before the film is released. Instead, use mystery toward the beginning of your speech that doesn't get solved until the end."

They Share Their Story. "Many speakers talk about how powerful stories are. But the difference between sharing your story and sharing a *certain part* of your story can make or break whether you get the outcomes you seek through your presentations. Instead of just generically sharing your story, mine out the unexpected moment that led to the insight you have to share with others."

They Provide Their Whole Framework. "Many speakers make their keynote presentation a breakdown of their whole system—often conveyed through a clever acronym. But forty-six of the fifty most popular TED talks offer one key idea that they can integrate right then and there. The audience can then take further steps to explore it afterward."

They Provide All Their Slide Content All At Once. "Bullet points on slides get a bad rap for being too distracting. But a savvy speaker will simply animate one component of their slides at a time to keep their audience with them throughout."

Confessions Of A TEDx Event Organizer

If you want to attract high-paying clients, it pays to speak. A speech that can generate credibility online is a TEDx Talk.

According to the website Ted.com, a TEDx Talk is a showcase for speakers presenting great, well-formed ideas in under eighteen minutes. The short talk format demands a speaker holds the audience's attention. Talks can be about a big idea, a tech demo, a talk about an issue, and even a talk about a small idea.

David W. Riggs has organized three TEDx events and coached thirty TEDx speakers.

"Connect with the conference organizer," says Riggs. "Every year we share a Google form for speakers to apply with and receive around one hundred applicants. Most of those applications fall to the wayside."

Riggs says those that get the most attention are the applicants that try to reach out to the organizer. The best way to do this is by using the TEDx page on the TED website to look up the event you'd like to apply to and see if the organizing team is listed at the bottom of the page.

If they are, find them on LinkedIn, Twitter, Instagram, or even contact them through their website, if they have one.

But the real secret is sixty seconds of video.

"Record a one-minute video introducing yourself," says Riggs. "Yes, I know what you're thinking, 'Do I really have to make a video?' Yes, yes you do."

Doing a video is not because the organizing team cares about what you look like or if you have the right lighting for a video.

"What we want to see is whether or not you're comfortable on camera," says Riggs. "A simple one-minute video that introduces yourself, your talk idea, and why you'd be a great fit for their event does wonders for your chances of being selected."

If the application form for the event you're applying to has the option to submit a video, then do it. If the form doesn't have that option, do whatever you can to get the organizing team that one-minute video.

"Find a talk that resembles yours," says Riggs. "As a TEDx Organizer, almost every decision I make comes back to one thing: how a prospective talk will affect the event. The same goes for you as an applicant. Whenever we review applications, we discuss how their talks will fit into the event."

Here's a little trick Riggs shares with clients to ensure their talk is interesting to the organizing team. First, go to YouTube and search for a TEDx talk and find one that interests you. This is your example to follow.

Once you've found one, analyze this example from top to bottom. You'll find that many talks utilize storytelling, attention-getting one-liners, and humor.

"So, when you fill out your application, talk about how you would also include stories, attention-getting one-liners, and humor. Bonus points if you share a few examples of what you plan to say," advises Riggs.

Getting booked to give a TEDx talk is hard, but not impossible. The hard is what makes it good to do.

Build Rapport Before You Take The Stage

Your job as a public speaker is not to just show up and throw up your PowerPoint. Your job is to make connections.

When done well, speaking can be the best way to attract high-paying clients. To repeat: when done well.

Debbie Peterson has presented to thousands of employees, leaders, and clients at various-sized organizations. She has learned a thing or two about connecting with an audience.

Peterson is a professional member of the National Speakers Association and the author of *CLARITY: How Smart Professionals Create Career Success on Their Terms.*[13] In addition to being paid to speak, her speeches help her find clients who want a career coach.

MAKE IT RAIN

 Peterson shared her top tips on how to build rapport with an audience before you take the stage:

Have a good recent headshot. "Have you ever seen a picture for an obituary that was clearly taken in high school? Well, speakers can be guilty of the same thing. This picture will be all over the event-marketing materials, and you want your audience to recognize you when you get there. If you've gone to a much different hairstyle, don't have to bother with hair anymore, started wearing contacts, or perhaps aged *more* than a bit, then you'll want to update your headshots."

Create a promotional video. "This is a way that your audience can get not only a glimpse of your content but of your style. This allows you to connect face to face without having arrived at the event yet.

Send a LinkedIn connection. "I get the pre-event roster from the meeting professional and send a LinkedIn request with a message telling them that I'm glad to be their keynote speaker for their upcoming event and that I'm looking forward to meeting them in person. I also give them a chance to ask a question related to my topic. The question allows you to connect with those in the audience that may be more introverted. A LinkedIn request is also not as invasive as sending an email and people are more likely to accept it."

Attend a pre-event function. "Usually, there is some sort of function in the evening before I speak. I'm there meeting people and getting to know more about them and their roles in their organization. It allows me to ask questions, get examples I can work into my presentation, and do a shout-out or two from stage which is an instant group rapport-building technique. I also, however, can ask for introductions to people within the organization that I might not be able to meet otherwise."

Work the room. "If I open the conference, I am down to the room early so I can go to breakfast, not to eat, but to casually work the room with my cup of coffee. I say hello, tell them how happy I am to be here, and tell them to let me know if they have any questions. If I'm on later in the day, then I do this at lunch too. Stand close to the door when people start to come in and say hi. People will begin to notice you."

If networking is good, being a speaker who builds rapport is the greatest networking opportunity to attract high-paying clients. While your content is important, ultimately it is the experience you create with the audience that serves you well.

MAKE IT RAIN

 By Henry DeVries

My books are my children, and like my children I expect them to support me in my old age. A book is a marketing tool and speaking about the book is a sales strategy. Here is a checklist of sixteen ways to speak to sell books (and find clients) that I have used:

- Small-scale seminars that you host with four to eight in attendance

- Private, invitation-only summits that you host with twelve to twenty-four in attendance

- Public seminars that you or others promote and charge admission to attend

- In-house paid workshops that pay you to present to one company only

- Local and national association meetings where you are a keynoter, breakout session speaker, panelist, or a roundtable moderator

- Radio and television shows and podcasts that interview you for how-to advice

- CEO peer group meetings like Vistage International (formerly TEC), Inner Circle, and Renaissance Forum

- College courses for adults and extended education programs, like the ones offered through university extension programs

- Public workshops that are fundraiser events that pay you a percentage of the gate

- Chamber of Commerce events, from monthly breakfasts to special seminars

- Teleseminars and webinars that you put on or that others invite you to speak at

- Promoter 50/50 seminars and expos where you are invited to speak and sell an information product, then split the proceeds with the person staging the event

- Prerecorded audio and video products that you sell on your website

- Service club speeches to groups like the Rotary Club and Lions Club

- Videos you make for YouTube

SECRET #7

Attract Clients With Podcasts

What is the secret of podcasting success? Ask a person who has reached three million listeners.

"Most podcasters quit before completing ten episodes. Don't quit," says podcasting expert Doug Sandler, a man who understands the value of persistence.

Doug Sandler knows that nothing can take the place of persistence in podcasting. As host of several shows including *The Nice Guys on Business* podcast, he and his cohost Strickland Bonner have gotten over three million downloads in more than 175 countries.

Doug Sandler is indeed a nice guy. His father was the late author David H. Sandler, creator of the Sandler Sales Methodology,[14] a man who advocated professionalism in sales.

"Launching a podcast is much more than just opening up a microphone, sharing your thoughts on a recorder, and distributing your message on Apple Podcasts," says Doug Sandler. "And yet, the majority of people that get into podcasting are clueless about the power they have in their hands if their launch, production, and strategy are in alignment."

Appearing as a guest on a podcast is a marketing gift that keeps giving. After being a guest on his show, an author asked Doug Sandler for his best advice for those considering podcasting as a strategy to attract high-paying clients.

"Know why you are getting into the podcasting space," advises Doug Sandler. "Pick a reason you are starting a show."

MAKE IT RAIN

 For those who want to build their impact and influence and put money in the bank, Doug Sandler offered three main goals for a podcast:

To build influence. "Build your show's ego," says Doug Sandler. "Invite guests on your show that are influencers in your space. By associating with other influencers, you become an influencer."

To grow your community. "Sharing your message and your content is key to building your community," says Sandler. "If you eventually want to provide a service or product through promotion on your podcast, you will need to build a community."

To make money. "If money is your motivation, do not be shy about it," says Sandler. "Focus on building your podcast like a business. In general, there are five ways to make money podcasting: advertising, brand sponsorships, selling your services to the community, donations, and turning guests into clients."

The bottom line: To attract high-paying clients you should actively seek guest spots on podcasts. This is earned media and it takes persistence.

How To Make Your Podcast Stand Out

Podcasting is not for everyone.

If you are going to podcast, be original or don't bother. That is the advice of Dusty Weis, whose podcast *Lead Balloon* was selected by *Adweek* to win their 2020 Marketing Podcast of the Year award.

Creating another boring, ho-hum podcast is a dusty road to failure.

"We have a failure problem in the fields of PR and marketing," says Weis. "Not the act of failure, but the fear of it. Failure has become so stigmatized, that many operations would rather embrace formulaic mediocrity than risk trying something new because of the fear that it might fail."

Should you not do a podcast because it might fail? Perhaps. In a podcast world with more than 1.75 million shows, Weis says you're not going to make waves doing what's already been done a thousand times before.

Be original. Be bold. Be interesting. As the late advertising great David Ogilvy said, you can't bore people into buying. Podcasting might not be expensive to do, but the opportunity cost of your time and energy is huge if you are podcasting to attract high-paying clients.

"When I launched the *Lead Balloon* podcast, I was putting my content-marketing-money-where-my-mouth-is on that imperative," says Weis. "My customers are PR and marketing practitioners, so I needed to make a show that appealed to them."

As he started to research the other shows in the PR and marketing genre, he was dumbfounded by the seemingly formulaic nature of so many of them. But why, he wondered, since this is a creative field and it's full of creative people.

"So, I turned hard into the imperative, 'Be Original, or Don't Bother,'" says Weis. "Where other marketing podcasters focus on quantity of content, I focus on quality. Where others do thought leadership, I do storytelling. Where others focus on accelerating their cadence, I spend forty to fifty hours getting an episode just right."

And above all, *Lead Balloon* celebrates learning through failure.

He knew *Lead Balloon* was finding an audience. Two-thirds of his revenue currently comes from clients who found him through *Lead Balloon*.

Being selected as *Adweek*'s Marketing Podcast of the Year was a game changer for Weis. He beat out agencies from around the world for that honor and he did it as a start-up, working from a home studio during Covid, in complete defiance of fear of failure.

"There are more outlets for your listeners' time and attention than there have ever been in human history," says Weis. "They give you their time and attention for free, and you owe it to them to provide them content that doesn't suck. You owe them the modest investment of money and expertise that it takes to make your podcast sound professional, and you owe them the time and the effort that it takes to come up with an original idea."

SECRET #8

Make Relationships If You Want To Get Help Making It Rain

There is a scary word to overcome if you want to attract high-paying clients.

"There's one particular word," Bob Paskins says, "that makes most consultants and professionals shudder and back away as if a skunk had just walked by. That word is: referrals."

Here's a truism about referrals: If you don't ask, you don't get.

Paskins is a Portland-based go-to expert in the areas of corporate sales, team building, account management, and customer service.

Paskins says, "We ask our friends for recommendations or referrals all the time:

'Where is a good Chinese restaurant?'

'We have a leak in our bathroom. Do you know a good plumber?'

'Where did you buy your last car and was it a good experience?'

Why don't we ask our clients for referrals as well?"

Why do people have such a negative reaction to the word referrals?

"In my experience, referrals are not only the easiest, but also the most enjoyable way to grow your business," says Paskins.

Many feel awkward asking a current client to refer potential clients. Why is that?

Paskins says, "When I ask people why they don't ask for referrals, I commonly get responses like these:

> 'Who would give me a referral in the first place?'

> 'I don't even know if my clients would be comfortable giving me a referral, so I don't feel comfortable in asking.'

> 'I'm sure this client is being asked for referrals all of the time, and I don't want to bother them by being yet another person asking them for a referral.'"

These are common excuses you have no doubt heard or said yourself.

"Clients *do* want to give you referrals," reasons Paskins. "I was able to triple my book of business when I learned to ask for referrals. Why is there such a taboo around asking for referrals?"

According to Paskins, we live in a work environment where your best clients want you to thrive with your business. They are pulling for you to succeed.

Referrals are too important to leave to chance. Half of your high-paying clients should be coming from referrals. Have no fear as you pursue referrals.

There are a few times that the likelihood of getting a referral is at its peak. Remember, there is a risk of giving a referral from your client's perspective, so you must position the dialogue in a way so that you do not diminish the quality of your relationship, and even in a way that enhances and strengthens that relationship.

First, some perspective. Asking for a referral is most likely a withdrawal from the emotional bank account with your client. Have you built up enough of a balance so that you have earned this right to make such a withdrawal? If you have not, then you risk shutting down that emotional bank account forever. Scott Love once knew a recruiter who asked for referrals from people she met over the phone. "My name is Gina and I'm a recruiter and I wanted to find out who you know who would be interested in this opportunity." Most people would say, "Sorry, I don't know anyone." That was it. It was a flat ask that had no thought put into it and ended up alienating her from people because it didn't connect with any value.

To earn the right to ask for referrals, look at ways that you can increase the value of the bank account so that you have enough of a balance to make such a withdrawal. Ways you can do this include building an authentic relationship over time. As you have earned the trust of others, you can see how that bank account balance has increased. When you have it, you can take a withdrawal from it and you don't risk the account shutting down. When you do it right, the act of asking for a referral can increase that balance.

Other ways of increasing the account balance beyond the normal ways of building a relationship include following up. Make sure your product or service is doing what it is supposed to do and that they are happy with their decision. This can also be a good time to ask for a referral as your client is reminded of the value.

MAKE IT RAIN

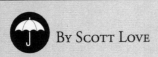 By Scott Love

Here are a few more ideas on how to keep that emotional bank account balance in your favor so you are more likely to get referrals. I suggest you take these action steps:

Thank them for their business. This is a natural conclusion to a service delivered and payment rendered. "Thank you for your business. It means a lot to me to help you in this way."

Anchor the moment. I usually do this when I place a partner at a firm. He or she just got the offer and accepted it. I anchor the emotion in a sincere conversation about how happy I am for him or her. "How exciting this must be for you!"

Ask for help. This may not be the right time for you to ask for a referral, but you can certainly ask for permission to ask for referrals. "I may reach out to you at some point to ask for help in terms of referrals. Would that be okay?" When they say yes, say, "Thank you, that means a lot to me."

When you ask for referrals, here are a few ideas:

Don't send out a mass email asking for referrals. It weakens the relationship.

Don't send out an individual email. That is, unless you and that person have already talked about your doing so.

Time the ask to coincide at a point when value is greatest. It's different for each offering. Some professionals should note that their clients have the highest value or perceived value right after the closing of the sale. For others it might be a few weeks or months later. If so, then schedule it in your calendar to follow up.

Don't ask it this way: "Do you know anyone?" Ask this: "Who do you know whom I can help in the same way I helped you?"

Ask if you can mention their name. In some scenarios, it may even help to ask them to introduce you to each other. "Could you do me a favor? Would you introduce us to each other by email?" This may be a larger ask, so make sure that you have put enough value in the equation so you can ask for this.

If you follow this formula and do a little bit each day, you'll see how much easier it is to fill your pipeline with high-quality leads that are all warm connections.

Expand Your Advocates And Develop Affiliates

There are four magic words in the English language: "I know a guy."

Referrals make a difference. You want to be the person they refer others to.

"If you deal with CEOs and other C-suite people, a sophisticated and nuanced referral approach is absolutely necessary," says Scott Hamilton, founder of the Executive Next Practices Institute,[15] a network of enterprise-level key executives. "With the C-suite, budget and RFPs are almost never an issue. It is a relationship-based sale that is fast-forwarded via the well-crafted referral."

First things first. Pandemic fatigue is not a medical condition, but the struggle is real. Did the pandemic make you feel like you swallowed a giant apathy pill? You are not alone. But you may not have recognized it as grief, especially if you and your loved ones have been fortunate enough to have maintained your health.

Grief is a natural response to loss. And when losses are intangible, such as loss of socializing, favorite experiences, or familiar habits, it's important to acknowledge them. But even more vital is to acknowledge what remains and what is possible.

When it comes to your business development needs, how do you find your way back from apathy, sadness, or isolation so you can grow your business? The first step is to get in the right mental framework. The second step is to cultivate your referral partners and stay in touch. In the prepandemic days, there was a proven strategy of having a coffee or lunch with potential referrals sources. In a time of social distancing, that is not a recommended strategy.

MAKE IT RAIN

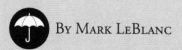 By Mark LeBlanc

Here are solid referral actions for the coming year:

Whip your CRM into shape first. Digitize your outreach with a customer relationship manager (CRM) program like Nimble. This is a simple, smart CRM for Office 365 and G-suite teams. You can automatically combine contacts, social media connections, inboxes, and calendar appointments. Some of its clients include GoDaddy, Coldwell Banker, and Upwork. This app allows you to tag a contact multiple times so you can easily make lists. However, do not just tag a referral as a referral. Are they an advocate or an affiliate?

Build a list of twenty-five advocates. Advocates are champions of you and your business who give you referrals for no monetary consideration. Advocates believe in you. An advocate likes to tell prospects that they do not receive any compensation for referring you; they just want the prospect to be well cared for. To make the advocate list there must be evidence of referring business to you. Why twenty-five? You should contact them on a regular basis, and more than twenty-five can become unwieldy. There is nothing wrong with giving small gifts to advocates to show your appreciation, but it cannot be a quid pro quo for every referral or every referral that becomes a client.

Build a list of twenty-five affiliates. Affiliates are people who will recommend you but expect a financial reward. To make the list they must agree to be willing to refer you for a fee. Typically, this might be in the form of a percentage, with 10 percent being a typical fee, but this will vary by industry. Some professionals, like attorneys, cannot pay referral fees. You should memorialize the agreement in writing, such as an email. This is not legal advice (I am not an attorney and do not give legal advice); this is practical because you should not rely on your memory.

Decide who you will be an advocate or an affiliate for. As you network, identify people who might make great referral sources. Start with this opener: "If you would be open to a conversation about being referral partners, that would be greatly appreciated." Starting with the word *if* is like a soft knock on the door.

Contact advocates and affiliates monthly. It is not the job of the advocates and affiliates to remember you; it is your job to remind them that you exist. Use a variety of means—do not just rely on email. Utilize other channels like texting, LinkedIn messages, Facebook messenger, and the telephone. Be brief because you want to be aware of their time.

Teach your advocates and affiliates your defining statement. My world changed forever the day I stumbled upon or was divinely guided to a new way to introduce myself at a networking meeting. In my book *Defining You: How Smart Professionals Craft the Answers to: Who Are You?*

What Do You Do? How Can You Help Me?[16] I teach the concept of the defining statement. Your defining statement is a simple answer to a simple question: What do you do, and who do you do it for? If your defining statement is conversational, you will use it and say it in the marketplace. It is similar but different from the typical elevator pitch meant to wow people. "Addressing a prospect's threat will get you in earlier in the process and at a higher level," says Bryan Gray, founder of Revenue Path Growth and author of the book *The Priority Sale*.[17] "The right defining statement can award you the next fifteen minutes of attention at the right level in an organization," says Gray.

Give if you want to get. If you want to receive referrals you need to give referrals. Let the law of reciprocation work in your favor. A place to start is to reach out and give specific recommendations on LinkedIn. Be honest and specific. You will be amazed at how many people want to return the favor.

Snail mail them little gifts to remind them you appreciate them. I have sent packets of seeds, baseball cards to wish them a happy spring, unusual paper clips, multicolored Post-it notes, and other items I find at a dollar store. Include a note expressing your gratitude. Many referral sources say they look forward to the lumpy envelopes I send.

Be ready with an email response. Chance favors the prepared. When someone sends a referral by email, I am ready with a preset response loaded into my signature files in MS Outlook. I send the email to the referrer and the prospect. I thank the referrer for the introduction, and I formally introduce myself in seven sentences and then provide a link to my calendar for a no-cost strategy call.

Offer up a template for an email they can send out about you. In mine, I mention the relationship and why they might want to get in touch with me. I make it easy for my advocates and affiliates to pass along my information.

Close the loop. Do your utmost to close the loop with the referrer to tell them what happened and that you appreciate the referral.

Here is the bottom line: The time has come to leave the grief of the pandemic behind and rededicate to solid business development strategies such as accelerating referrals.

News Flash: It Really Is All About Relationships

"So, it's not gonna be easy. It's gonna be really hard. We're gonna have to work at this every day…"

–Young Noah (Ryan Gosling), in the film *The Notebook*

Do you want to succeed in attracting high-paying clients? Focus on building relationships, and the sales will follow.

To learn more about the importance of relationship-building to attract high-paying clients, I spoke with Deb Brown Maher, whose professional background spans over thirty years of expertise in all levels of sales execution, training, and consulting.

She has worked with companies that include Hershey Chocolate, Lucent Technologies, Comcast Cable, Dell, CA (Computer Associates) and AMP (now Tyco).

"Most business owners start their business because of a passion for their product or service, not because they want to sell," says Maher. "The role of selling has a negative connotation because we've all endured interacting with unskilled salespeople."

Success at sales, says Maher, begins with a mindset, or attitude, toward what you sell and how you sell it, because attitudes drive behavior.

"There are two fundamental sales attitudes—polar opposites—that drive sales behaviors; one values short-term relationships, and the other values long-term relationships," says Maher.

So, what differentiates these two attitudes from each other?

"The driving attitude behind short-term sales relationships is that the sale must be made during the first contact, or it won't happen. This sales strategy teaches various high-pressure tactics, doing whatever it takes to make the sale immediately. There is no system for following up; salespeople simply walk away from any lead that says no, moving on to the next. This short-term relationship approach often results in viable leads not buying because they feel they've been treated disrespectfully. The 'churn' approach is also contingent upon having enough marketing dollars to generate new leads continually, while ignoring the segment who might have bought in the future but are lost because there's no follow-up."

And the more long-term approach?

"Contrast prioritizing the short term with valuing long-term relationship building. This approach seeks to truly understand what's important to the buyer through meaningful dialogue guided by questions asked and actively listening to the buyer's responses. Here the buyer is respected as the decision maker, who is in complete control of whether and when they buy, or not."

According to Maher, regardless of what you sell, applying more diligent, long-term relationship-building strategies will increase your bottom line in two ways: "Building trust results in more sales, and reducing lead generation costs by maximizing the leads you already have."

SECRET #9

Use Key Influencers To Generate Word-Of-Mouth Advertising

I f you want to attract high-paying clients, you do not need to have a multimillion-dollar marketing budget. Spend time helping your key influencers understand the value of your solution and watch the word spread like wildfire.

That's the view of rainmaker Sande Golgart, president of Zonez, who took the company from survive to thrive during the pandemic. Golgart is often quoted on real estate issues and trends affecting businesses from start-ups to the Global 1000. He has been featured on *Fox Business News*, *ABC News*, and various other media outlets.

As a small service business whose primary focus is helping companies create highly productive office environments, the lockdown of March 2020 felt like a death sentence. "We knew the world would forever be changed," said Golgart. "We had to take action quickly if we were going to survive—let alone thrive."

He immediately launched a research effort to understand the biggest issues companies would need to address when they returned to the office. The research was clear and consistent: companies would need to find a way to separate people and clean the air in the workplace.

"We went to work with our engineers and staff and created the world's only blocking and air filtration system that captures and filters the air at the source where it is exhaled, coughed, or sneezed into a shared environment," said Golgart. "We spent countless hours problem solving until we had developed a viable solution to the problem we uncovered. In July 2020, we launched our new brand, Clean Zonez."

MAKE IT RAIN

 Here are four tips from Golgart on how to leverage key influencers:

Tip #1: Focus on what you have. Do not get consumed with what you do not have. "We had no budget and no extra money to invest in expensive advertising. Additionally, we did not have a big team that could knock on doors and tell our story. What we did have were strong relationships built over time and a reputation for delivering high-quality, well-engineered products. We decided that our best option was to invest in the relationships with those who had the most credibility and experience, with the largest spheres of influence."

Tip #2: Take inventory of the potential influence you can create. "Make a list of your trusted relationships with businesses and connections that have the largest degree of influence. Quantify the degree of influence each trusted relationship has and create a priority list. Influence can be the number of years someone has been in business (credibility). It can also be the number of customers or contacts they have."

Tip #3: Invest your time and effort where you are likely to see the biggest returns. "Time is limited. No one has time to do things that are not impactful. You must have the discipline to invest only in people and activities that can generate the biggest returns. For us, we turned to key influencers, such as Gibson Office Products, which has locations in New York, New Jersey, and Florida and more than seventy-five years of experience selling commercial office furnishings to the largest companies in their markets. Gibson executives were able to make introductions to Prologis, the largest industrial real estate company in the world. As of December 31, 2019, the company owned 3,840 buildings, comprising 814 million square feet in nineteen countries. Prologis is now offering the Clean Zonez solutions to all its tenants. Next, we turned to Connection Resource in the Bay Area, which has a stellar reputation for helping the Bay Area's largest corporations, such as Google, Facebook, and Apple. Additionally, we spent time educating IWG executives on the benefits of Clean Zonez; IWG operates the world's largest shared office network, serving over 2.5 million individual companies."

Tip #4: Help your key influencers understand the impact they can make. "Invest quality time with these key relationships, ensuring they understand the full value of the solution and what it can mean for their business. Once these key influencers understood how uniquely impactful the Clean Zonez product was, they quickly shared the information with their networks."

The bottom line: In a matter of weeks, his new service was known by the largest customers, accompanied by the endorsements of trusted influencers. Never underestimate the power of word-of-mouth advertising. And never assume it just happens on its own.

SECRET #10

Monopolize The Listening

magine this scenario: The prospective client has answered your questions and told you their problem. What do you do next?

If you answered, "start closing," please go to the back of the class. There is a much better way for attracting high-paying clients to enroll with you.

First, sell nothing. Instead, prove you listened. That's the advice of a sales coach who has been on 30,000 face-to-face sales calls.

"Years ago, I started repeating back what they want and why they wanted it to them for clarity," says sales expert Joe Pallo. "It did clarify things, but it did a lot more."

Don't be a typical salesperson if you want to land more high-paying clients. That's probably music to the ears of most professionals and consultants because they abhor the idea of being thought of as a salesperson.

By selling nothing before repeating back what the prospects say, Pallo reports the following things happened:

- It showed that he listened to them.

- It showed that they are important.

- It showed that he was on their side.

- It confirmed their thinking in their own minds.

- It created a buying atmosphere.

- It helped prospects to like him a bit more.

- It sucked all of the "pressure close" out of the room.

- It showed that he understood them.

These are all great outcomes that build rapport and increase closing rates.

"Most importantly it allowed me to sell what they wanted to buy, versus selling what I wanted to sell," said Pallo. "Often, I heard, 'Joe, you said it better than I did.' What a great spot to be in and I haven't even started my pitch."

What Pallo did was really listen to the prospect and prove it to them.

Pallo has been selling for decades. He financed his college education by selling books door-to-door for the Southwestern Company of Nashville, Tennessee. Years later he became a sales trainer with the Tom James Company and worked with numerous start-ups and family-run businesses.

In 2017, Pallo took his own advice and started his own company, Sell Nothing, LLC. As a sales coach, he focuses on making sure that the basic sales principles are understood and implemented.

"Two words are probably the most valuable in sales and are underused: What else?" says Pallo. "Asking 'what else?' forces prospects to add to their answer, paint a better picture, and create a better understanding."

In building a relationship, Pallo says whoever is talking is buying. If you are talking more than the prospect is, you are buying their objections. Discoveries in neuroscience prove decision-making is largely emotional, not logical.[18]

"Emotions are weird, fickle things that are constantly changing," says Pallo. "In a sense, they are nothing. Selling nothing is purely an emotional sale. What they want is important, but why they want it is even more important."

Bottom line: Never pitch until the prospects have told you what they want and why they want it. Prove you heard and understood. Active listening builds trust, the real key to building a relationship with a client.[19]

GLASBERGEN

"If you know how to beg, we may have a position for you in Accounts Receivable."

SECRET #11

How To Convert Prospects Into Clients

The goal of generating leads is to have a meaningful conversation. The goal of the meaningful conversation phase is to build a case for prospects to make an informed decision, even before they know what you charge. Depending on the type of sale or the complexity of the transaction, this phase can take thirty minutes to an hour or more. In a complex sale, it may require a series of conversations, steps, and a proposal or discussion document.

The traditional book or course on selling would include a section on uncovering and overcoming objections using clever closing comebacks. Forget everything you learned about this type of selling. Those processes, tips, tricks, and tactics are worn out and tired. Your prospects are smarter today and repelled by these types of techniques. Stick to the facts. Seek understanding. Learn how to navigate this phase as a skilled surgeon would perform a delicate operation.

Share the truth about what you can and cannot provide. Develop a sense of conviction about what you will do and how you can best be of service. Articulation is everything. Rely less on your tools and more on being present with your prospects. When you build a better case for them, you can trust the decisions your prospects make. You are less likely to feel rejected if it doesn't go your way. Let your prospects make the best answer for them on their timeframe. Honor your prospects and they will turn into enthusiastic customers or clients for life.

MAKE IT RAIN

 By Mark LeBlanc

After coaching more than one thousand rainmakers, I have learned some valuable truths about questions.

The following questions make up the skeleton of a meaningful conversation. No two are created equal; however, with a solid framework and proven track record, your ratio of rainmaking wins to losses will increase. More specifically, your ratio of wins to losses with right-fit or perfect-fit prospects will increase. This framework will allow you to develop your skills over time and give you a way to debrief a conversation to improve it.

Here are examples of questions the most successful rainmakers use:

Question #1: How long have you been thinking about buying this service?

Question #2: What is your timeframe for making your decision or target date for delivery or completion?

Question #3: How come you find yourself in this situation? Tell me a little more about…

Question #4: Are you presently talking with anyone else who provides these types of services?

These questions will help you zero in on a prospect's needs and wants. In addition, you may uncover an obstacle or two that could get in the way of doing business. It is always better to find out sooner rather than later.

Navigate The Decision Phase

After you have built your case with a prospect, you have every right to ask two simple questions. I refer to these two questions as the courage questions:

Clarification question

1. Does this make sense?

   Have I been clear?

   Is this what you are interested in?

Enrollment question

2. Would you like to work with me?

   Do you feel it is a good fit for us to work together?

   Would you like me to prepare an outline of how we might approach working together?

"Does anyone have a *better* idea?"

SECRET #12

The Greatest Rainmaking Strategy In The World: Thought Leadership

Honestly, we find business development success is about thought leadership," says Rob Sher, CEO of The One Page Business Plan Company.

Successful rainmakers at professional service firms confide to me repeatedly that a book is the number one business development tool and talking about the book is the number one business development strategy. Leveraging the book to speak, even virtually through webinars and podcast interviews, is a secret weapon.

Sher credits thought leadership to the firm's late founder, author Jim Horan, and his own two books, for turbocharging rainmaking success on all fronts at his company. Horan's bestselling book, *The One Page Business Plan*,[20] sparked a revolution in how corporate America, nonprofit organizations, and even independent professionals approach planning.

Successful rainmaking is about persistence, says Sher.

"It can be disheartening doing a webinar and not landing dozens of clients right away," says Sher. "It may bring no immediate clients. But then a year later someone who heard you calls and says, 'I want to buy.' So many people give up too early. I don't think they fully understand that it's a long game."

The One Page Business Plan Company is an international consulting firm specializing in planning and performance management systems. The company has over five hundred licensed consultants worldwide. According to Sher, its innovative web-based planning and performance management tools "are rapidly becoming the tools of choice for CEOs."

Before becoming CEO after the death of Horan in 2019, Sher was a top 1 percent One Page Business Plan consultant for over eight years, Sher has written two books, *Mighty Midsized Companies: How Leaders Overcome 7 Silent Growth Killers* and *The Feel Of The Deal*,[21] and is a regular columnist on leadership for Forbes.com.

Building relationships with potential clients, a rainmaking approach nicknamed The Trojan Horse Strategy, is something Sher discovered as a happy accident.

"My second book, *Mighty Midsized Companies*, was research-based," says Sher. "I interviewed 110 different companies, of which two became very large clients by accident. That is because I was asking good questions for the research and focused on midsized companies, which were my target consulting clients."

Sher says rainmaking is hard work and it takes perseverance to make it pay.

"Business development success is about doggedly mixing a variety of business development tactics across the spectrum. So, it's touching through writing, touching through speaking, and 'picking up the damn phone' as Jim Horan liked to say."

In the coming year Sher's company plans to decrease spending on search engine optimization (SEO) for its website and improving its customer relationship management (CRM). In other words, generating fewer leads through SEO and then wasting less of the leads generated through other sources.

"The number one thing working for us at The One Page Plan Company is building and improving the series of activities that help filter through people who show initial interest," says Sher. "We're doing a lot of improvement in gathering prospects. I also have to say that we're working hard on diligent use of a CRM. Carefully following up with all our outreach tools so that we don't leave leads unturned, but on the other hand, not overworking them and wasting their time and ours."

"Sometimes you have to treat
them like a *dysfunctional* family."

SECRET #13

Build A Network If You Don't Have One

This is a comeback story, a rebirth of a career by a career expert.

"I did something really stupid about ten years ago," said career thought leader Brenda Abdilla. "I told my consulting clients that I was changing my business model and then I shut down all aspects of my business except for the executive coaching part."

Abdilla is a respected and sought-after career and leadership coach.

Today she works with corporate leaders who want more effective strategies for team accountability and collaboration, and with professionals who are navigating a change in their high-level careers. In fact, more than 90 percent of her coaching clients get promoted, land the role they desire, or address their core issue within twelve months of engaging her.

But there was a time of struggle.

"As I said goodbye to the business that earned me six figures as a speaker, trainer, recruiter, and occasionally as a coach, I eagerly began to network in my local market," said Abdilla. "Guess what happened next?"

Nothing.

"It was alarming to realize that I had no professional credibility in my local market, the greater Denver area," said Abdilla. "I quickly realized that I had never really taken the time to develop my local network since my consulting clients were all over the country/world."

MAKE IT RAIN

Abdilla can now say she has a thriving business and truly loves her work and her clients. Here are the three strategies she used to build her network and acquire ideal clients:

Work for free until you can work for a fee. "This is an old adage I learned as a pro speaker and it works," says Abdilla. "As you meet people and make professional connections, offer to do your work for free in the form of workshops, lunch-and-learns, presentations, etc. Unless you prefer to cold call and collect rejections, this method will work, but it takes time. Put together a one-to-three-hour program with your best material and offer it for free or a very low fee to your budding network. You won't have to stay in the free zone for long if you really deliver. This concept works well if you are trying a newly added service to your business as well."

For example, a few years into her executive coaching business Abdilla decided to add career coaching to her services, which was serving a different market entirely. So, she put together a super-low-priced package and got a few clients to try it out. It was a hit.

"My current fee for that segment is approximately twenty-two times what that initial package cost my first few test clients," says Abdilla.

Stop thinking in terms of competition. Abdilla says: "If you think that you will build your network by connecting only with potential customers, you are going to need to expand your thinking in a big way. The way a thriving network can build your business is through partnerships, resources, and alliances—and none of those will come from your clients or potential clients. As you are building your network you will want to include people who are in the same space as you are and have an abundance mindset. For example, I am in two different mastermind groups with people who specialize in the same type of coaching I do. In the past month alone people from those groups have given me ideas, invited me to be a guest on their podcasts, and even a referral for a client. And of course, I do the same for them."

Be impeccable with your craft. "When we feel desperate, we tend to focus more on business acquisition than on excellence and impeccability in our craft. If you want to build a network where one does not exist it needs to be the other way around. First, you must serve; get results for clients; differentiate yourself by truly delivering. Stop trying to convince people of your excellence and show it instead. Otherwise, you are just part of the noise. Don't waste your money on a drip campaign or try a shortcut that promises to make you the overnight guru. Get back to work perfecting your craft on real people."

The bottom line: One of our favorite networking authors, Harvey Mackay, says we need to "dig our well before we are thirsty."[22] In our studies on business development, two of the top five ways to attract high-paying clients involve networking. The secret weapon for attracting new clients: relationships.

SECRET #14

Improve Your Voice Like Jeff, Tony, Gwen, And Angelina

I f you want to attract more high-paying clients, you need to speak better than you do now.

No doubt about it, prospects judge you on many factors, and one is on the quality of your voice. If you want to attract high-paying clients, you should pay attention to your voice.

If you want more vocal power, Love might be the answer.

Roger Love is Hollywood's go-to guy when it comes to voice. His client list includes notables such as Tony Robbins, Gwen Stefani, Jeff Bridges, Selena Gomez, and Bradley Cooper, among others.

He is arguably one of the world's leading authorities in voice and speech training. Perhaps no other vocal coach in history has been more commercially successful in both the speaking and singing fields.

Here's one noteworthy Hollywood credit. Love vocal coached Reese Witherspoon and Joaquin Phoenix for the film *Walk the Line.* The film received three Golden Globe Awards, one Screen Actors Guild Award, one Platinum Selling CD Award, a Grammy Award, and an Academy Award.

MAKE IT RAIN

To master vocal power is a lifelong pursuit. But how can you get started on the journey? Here are some quick tips Love shared for improving your vocal power:

Warm Up Your Voice. "A runner would never start a race without stretching before. Give your voice some stretching, too."

Drop Your Jaw Down. "Most people simply do not open their mouths enough to let the sound come out unobstructed."

Drink More Water. "You should drink about one-half gallon of pure water daily."

Wean Yourself Off Whispering. "When you whisper, you force a tremendous amount of extra air over the vocal cords making them dry and irritated."

Stop Tightening Your Abdomen. "Too many people hear the word 'support' from singing coaches and think it means to create pressure in your abdomen as a means to somehow push more sound out."

Learn Diaphragmatic Breathing. "It is very easy and much healthier for the body. Just put your hand on your abdomen, near your belly button. When you inhale, pretend that you have a balloon in there and let it expand. Then when you speak or sing, let it come back in."

Tea With Honey and Lemon Is a Bad Idea. "Hot, caffeinated tea with honey and lemon is a recipe for poor singing and speaking. Have you noticed how your fingers look like prunes when you take a long hot bath? Drinking very hot tea can take a similar toll on your throat."

Love has vocally produced more than 100 million-unit sales worldwide, written three top-selling books, created the best-selling audio programs *Vocal Power* and *The Perfect Voice*, and has appeared as a regular in four major network TV shows. His film voice coaching credits include *Walk the Line, Crazy Heart, Begin Again*, and *A Star Is Born*.

How To Vocalize Like A Boss The Arthur Samuel Joseph Way

Do you know what perhaps is the most powerful and underutilized tool you have in your life and your business? Would it surprise you to know it is your voice?

Arthur Samuel Joseph's mission is "to change the world through voice." He has taught globally for over five decades, and his client roster is a Who's Who of celebrities and business leaders.

"When we own our voice, we own our power," says Joseph.

No one knows how to leverage voice better than Joseph. His client list includes Angelina Jolie, Pierce Brosnan, Magic Johnson, Tony Robbins, Arnold Schwarzenegger, and NFL Commissioner Roger Goodell, just to name a few.

He has trained broadcasters at the NFL, NBA, MLB, ESPN, Fox, ABC, CBS, and NBC, as well as business leaders at Disney, Toyota, Ritz-Carlton, Deloitte, Ernst & Young, and the Federal Reserve Bank, among others.

Joseph is a masterful storyteller, a skill that he teaches to his students. Some of the other elements he teaches include body language, verbal and nonverbal expression, breathing techniques, vocal projection, and of course, vocal quality.

"Research proves that the greatest impact speakers have in any conversation comes not only from the words they say but from the sound of their voices," Joseph told me in an interview in his Southern California studio. "In other words, it is not just the message but the messenger that matters."

MAKE IT RAIN

 By Henry DeVries

In his fifth book, *Vocal Leadership: 7 Minutes a Day to Communication Mastery*,[23] Joseph shares all his secrets to what he terms Communication Mastery. The audiobook (read by the author) and print version of *Vocal Leadership* changed the trajectory of my speaking career and receives my highest recommendation, as do all his books and training products. I have purchased his books by the case and gift them to authors who want more impact and influence.

His trademarked Vocal Leadership method provides proven techniques and daily exercises to help any leader develop a commanding voice and presence. The book clearly instructs how to improve vocal quality, body language, and self-esteem to dramatically increase your influence. We recommend the audiobook version, so you can hear Joseph take you step-by-step through the process of becoming a more effective and commanding speaker.

And when I say speaker, I am not talking just from the speaking platform. Joseph teaches how to be in mastery in every conversation, public address, and personal encounter, from speeches to hundreds to sales meetings and presentations to a handful of people. In fact, being authentic in every communication, including one-on-one meetings, is a cornerstone of the process.

Formerly on the faculty of the University of Southern California School of Theatre, Joseph has been a visiting artist at Yale and George Washington Universities, and a guest lecturer at New York University.

Additionally, the internet has provided many opportunities to offer his proprietary Vocal Awareness training through his website, www. vocalawareness.com.

Joseph is especially enthusiastic about his certification program that is training a team of Certified Vocal Awareness Teachers. This is his legacy project to continue the mission of changing the world through voice.

Telepathic Telemarketing

SECRET #15

Consider A Side Hustle Like This One That Earned 40X ROI

I n my travels, I have the opportunity to work with the best and the brightest in the construction industry. I also get the opportunity to work with some real knuckleheads," says Nic Bittle. Those knuckleheads gave him an idea for a new book that produced a 4,000 percent return on investment.

Bittle, who lives in the little farm town of Corn, Oklahoma, is booked solid traveling the nation helping contractors through presentations, workshops, and tools he has developed that are designed to support the foreman learning process.

Before he published his new side hustle book, Bittle's then nine-year-old son Cruze, who was making money with his own side hustles like raising calves and selling honey, asked Dad to explain the concept of investing.

"Cruze had a pretty solid handle on earning, but saving was his downfall," said Bittle. "Cruze likes buying Legos, knives, and extra snacks at ballgames. I explained how I have invested some of my savings in the different books I have written. I grabbed a copy of one of my books and explained how much it cost to have it printed and every time I sell a copy, I get a return on my investment. I also explained there is a risk to every investment. There are no guarantees."

Bittle was already the author of the book *Good Foreman, Bad Foreman*.[24] "The book is for good foremen who want to become better leaders," says Bittle, who runs a company called Work Force Pro that helps contractors who want to prepare and develop their workforce to lead with impact.

Cruze made an offer to invest his savings in his dad's next book. That was a shrewd move.

Through the years Bittle often heard foremen complain about the new generation of apprentices. So, he decided to do a survey of his workshop attendees and asked 10,000 foremen the following three questions:

1. What one piece of advice would you give someone entering this industry?

2. What training do our apprentices most desperately need that they are not already receiving?

3. What one decision did you make that had the most significant impact on your life and career?

"The thousands of foremen and leaders in my workshops have told me it is the simple things about the business the apprentices are failing at," says Bittle. "The common-sense stuff that is not all that common anymore is where those who the foremen lead need to step it up."

Bittle knew apprentice training programs are typically thirty-six weeks in length. He determined from the survey the most needed subjects and turned it into thirty-six chapters. He also produced a companion video curriculum.

Bittle titled his 174-page book *Know This, Do That.*[25] The book is for those who want to go from apprentice to journeyman. He says it is the field guide for every apprentice who wants to put ideas into action and make them stick.

"The book is filled with the advice of those who have been there, who have walked the halls of the apprentice programs, those who, through their blood, sweat, and tears, have built a successful career and a life worth living in this industry," says Bittle.

Bittle targeted 658 union construction apprenticeship programs in the country. He mailed copies of the book with a Post-it Note that said: "Check out this book and video curriculum that can help change the way our apprentices look at their career." He sent 355 follow-up emails and made 242 phone calls.

While he got 625 no answers, he also got thirty-three yes answers for a 5 percent response rate.

"Some people think rejection doesn't bother me; it does," says Bittle. "But rejection doesn't stop me."

Apprenticeship programs started ordering books by the cases. More importantly, the investment produced a 40x return (4,000 percent ROI) through book and video sales. This translates to a six-figure return.

Bittle asks these questions in his book: "How are you investing in your career? How are you investing in yourself? How are you investing in others?"

For years we have documented similar cases of consultant book efforts resulting in returns of 400 percent to 2,000 percent ROI. Bittle's little book *Know This, Do That* is the record setter. More impressive, it's a leverage play because Bittle did not have to make money traveling the country giving more workshops.

"Cruze is now twelve and seeing a nice return on his investment," says Bittle, "although I don't think I am going to let him spend it all on Legos, knives, and snacks."

SECRET #16

Fire 90 Percent Of Your Clients

Say goodbye to the bad fits so you can say hello to more good fits.

Clients need to be treated fairly, not equally. And many should be shown out the door, even during the harsh COVID-19 economy.

That's the contrarian opinion of Martin Jacobs, a senior leader in the technology industry with more than twenty-five years of experience working internationally for both family-owned businesses and Fortune 500 companies such as Avnet and Texas Instruments.

Because of COVID-19 and the worldwide fear of a prolonged recession, many are tempted to take any clients they can find. Jacobs advocates a client-centric approach that favors your most profitable customers.

"These historical, unprecedented times call for strategies you probably didn't learn at business school," said Jacobs, an alum of the Wharton School of Business. "Surviving means implementing actions that at first might appear counter-intuitive."

MAKE IT RAIN

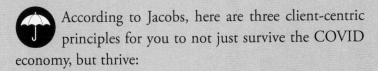 According to Jacobs, here are three client-centric principles for you to not just survive the COVID economy, but thrive:

Principle #1. Know that giving excellent customer service to everyone might be ruining your business. "If you are a business that boasts, 'We have great customer service! All our customers love us,' you'll have a problem surviving this new world economy," says Jacobs. "Great customer service to *all* of your customers can actually be the worst possible thing you do for your business and increase your chances of going bankrupt. This one-size-fits-all approach confuses customer service with customer-centricity. Customer-centricity is all about scaling your operations according to the value of a customer's returns.

Principle #2. Unless you are Amazon, limit small orders. "If 90 percent of your profit comes from your top clients, you dilute your profits and energy pursuing everybody else," says Jacobs. "Trying to please everyone will decrease your productivity, burn out your sales staff, and jeopardize losing your largest clients. Your largest customers go where they get the best treatment. And every order you take from a small customer takes away resources from your top customers. Therefore, find a business model for your small customers that provides pure profits for you. There are plenty of companies out there eager to sell your products for a commission. The commission takes away from your profit margins but eliminates all other downsides."

Principle #3. Give your top clients their own ringtone.
"Create loyalty by giving your top clients VIP treatment,"
says Jacobs. "At an executive retreat, after a few glasses of
wine, a CEO of a Silicon Valley-based company shared his
struggles with his marriage. That his successful business put
his family on the back burner and now he was going to lose
his family. From my own mistakes, I shared how I learned
how we could drive people most important to us away
when we do not set clear priorities. A different ringtone
might just do the trick."

The challenge many business leaders face today is a willingness to take
any client on regardless of the profit margin. The leader may feel sorry
for those clients who are also struggling with the recession. This can be
a shortsighted approach.

"Tough times, just like the one we have all been experiencing, show you
who your most loyal partners are," says Jacobs. "Pay proper attention
to these relationships and the COVID economy can just be a bump in
the road."

PART III

WHAT COMES NEXT?

SECRET #17

Build A Rainmaker Culture

There is a pattern in nature that has existed since the dawn of time, and you probably see this pattern each day without awareness of the formula behind it. You see it in ancient ammonite shells, living creatures, and flowers. It's called the Fibonacci sequence, and it's a spiraling rate of expansion that continues outward by about 30 percent with each rotation. It's even the reason why we perceive a smile to be an attractive thing.

Mathematically, this sequence is a series starting with 1 and 1, and each succeeding number is the sum of the two immediately preceding. 1+1 =2, 1+2=3, 2+3=5, 3+5=8, 5+8=13, etc.

So, the sequence looks like this: 1, 1, 2, 3, 5, 8, 13, 21, 34, etc.

Could this mathematical series give us insight into how to make more sales? Could we possibly unlock the secret of more sales by considering this formula? Can we turn our job in client development into the opportunity of a lifetime by understanding the growth concepts behind this sequence?

Think of it like this. Consider constant and active growth as one of the main attributes of those who are successful in client development. They never give up, they are always striving for one more call, and they are assertive in overcoming that "no" and turning it to a "yes" and doing so in a way that draws their prospect closer to them.

Here are three specific ways that this concept can help you generate more business.

Consider that this rate of expansion in the Fibonacci sequence is about 30 percent with each rotation.

MAKE IT RAIN

 By Scott Love

We challenge you to spend one hour a day in personal development. If you spent an hour each day in personal development, how much more powerful would you be in one year's time?

Here is how you do this. Take wasted time and turn it into money time. When you are driving in your commute, listen to a podcast or an audiobook on rainmaking or some other business development topic. If you have a half-hour commute each way, you are reclaiming that time and turning it into money-making time.

When I am on the elliptical or the treadmill for a half hour, I am halfway to my one-hour goal of development since I am also improving my health. So, if you do this and you listen to a thirty-minute audio sales podcast, you are doubling down. You realize one hour's worth of value in just a half-hour unit of time.

Look for little minutes here and there. Leave a few books scattered throughout the house. Have a few audio programs queued up on your iPhone ready to go at a moment's notice.

I also believe in becoming a good finisher. Even though you might have three books scattered in your house here and there, focus on completing at least one book a month. Books on sales, marketing, business, personal development, communication, personal finance, and personal relationships are always valuable.

Here are a few books I recommend that you start with.

Think Big, Act Bigger: The Rewards of Being Relentless, by Jeff Hayzlett

Smart Calling: How to Take the Fear, Failure and Rejection Out of Cold Calling, by Art Sobczak

Your Own Worst Enemy: Breaking the Habit of Adult Underachievement, by Ken Christian

Build Your Consulting Practice, by Henry DeVries and Mark LeBlanc

Client Attraction, Chain Reaction, by Henry DeVries

You will find that this daily diet of inspiration and discipline will be something you look forward to. Perhaps you used to do this. I'd recommend you do this again and keep at it. Create habits in building your knowledge with information that is inspiring and helps you close more sales.

Last year I spoke at a large national staffing agency's annual meeting. After my presentation, one of the sales representatives came up to me and told me she had a hard time becoming disciplined in her work. I asked her to describe this. She said, "I'm having a hard time just starting and staying with the activities I know I need to do to become successful."

I then asked her about her income goal. "What is your potential in terms of earnings, assuming you worked consistently at your peak performance level every hour of every day for a month?"

She replied, "If I do what I am supposed to do each hour of each day, I can earn $8,000 a month. That's my potential." I challenged her on that. I asked her if she really thought she could do this, and she confirmed that she honestly believed she had the potential to earn this kind of income.

I asked her to break it down into bite-sized daily targets. I asked her what activities she needed to do every day to hit that goal. She told me that based on their metrics, if she made thirty connection attempts a day over the phone, then she would earn around $8,000 each month. I set it up this way. "Suppose your boss wrote a check for you for

$8,000 on the first of the month and signed it and post-dated it for the 31st of the month. He told you that all you had to do was make the thirty calls a day and if you did that you could cash the check. Could you do that?"

"Absolutely!" she said.

Sometimes it's not the discipline but the drive and belief we need to have first to do the hard work of facing our fears. We can break down the monthly goal into daily bite-sized steps and focus on those small steps in front of us. If we do that, the work seems to be less intimidating. Her belief in staying disciplined was a longer stretch than in accomplishing the daily tasks if there was the promise of a specific reward.

How can you break your monthly revenue goal and income goal into specific daily tasks? What are those action steps (input) that lead up to sales (output)? These are called Key Performance Indicators, and if you focus on achieving a daily habit of a certain indicator (number of sales calls or pitch meetings, phone time, interviews, start dates, etc.), then eventually you will hit your output. This is a basic concept in management and it's something you have heard before. It never ceases to amaze me how simple this concept is yet how so many people neglect focusing on it. If you are in a business development role, then you should start managing yourself in this regard, because you are responsible for everything that happens to you.

The Fibonacci sequence is a constant reminder of paying attention to where you need to grow. At the end of every day, write down two things:

your greatest achievement and your biggest lesson learned. What is more relevant are the lessons that you learn each day. The achievements are reminders that you have what it takes to make those tough calls and get those large accounts and serves as a "replay mechanism" to help you build your confidence. The lessons learned serve as a data tool to help you build awareness of where you need to improve. Keep this document and review it every quarter. Pay attention to mistakes that you keep making. This data over time is subtle, but if you document it every day, you see patterns, and these patterns show you where you need to grow.

With the awareness of areas to improve, habits and rituals to help you overcome your fears, and the motivation to seize the day, you'll be well on your way to growing at least 30 percent a year in not just your business development activities, but in other areas of your life that are important to you. And that is the opportunity of a lifetime.

MAKE IT RAIN

 By Scott Love

I believe it's possible to continue to grow at a consistent pace each day by using rituals and habits as a motivating force to propel you forward. Rituals and habits are the forces that carry you forward in a state of performance regardless of how you feel.

Sometimes I don't feel like picking up the phone—which seems to weigh forty pounds—and making new connections with people. Hence, I rely on rituals to help me get through that almost daily hesitation and give me energy so that eventually I make calls and feel like making connections again. I hope that you can apply some of these ideas about rituals and habits to your own life. I'll share with you what I do and perhaps you can find some ideas and modify them, so they fit what is important to you.

When I wake up, I make my bed. Your mother was right. This daily habit separates night from day. It's a line of demarcation that tells you there is a new day and that you are beginning to face it with action. Action always dissipates fear.

I then say to myself, out loud even, a series of mantras. A mantra is a phrase that changes your emotional state. This is a common attribute of those who are high achievers in sports. High-performing athletes know that their performance on the field is a byproduct of their state, meaning the state of their emotions. They know that changing how they feel changes their results. Some of these mantras may seem trite and even silly, but I'd recommend withholding judgment until you test them and see what it does for you. Try these mantras for a week as your daily rituals and see what happens to your emotional state and your performance:

"Today is going to be the most exciting day of my life."

"Everything I touch turns to gold."

"Everybody I talk to wants to do business with me."

"Put me in the path of those whom I can serve."

This fourth mantra is almost like a prayer and serves as a reminder that the only way I can create income through business development is by taking my eyes off myself and serving others.

When I get to my office, I make one phone call before I do anything else. For people who are in the business of making new connections, there is a causal relationship between making connections over the phone with real live human beings (phone time) and success. Sometimes professionals hide behind social media as an excuse not to make reach-outs. I'm not talking about cold reach-outs, but making legitimate bona fide connections with existing clients, people who know you, or referrals. Using social media as a way to connect with people is not the silver bullet in the world of client development, even though it can raise your profile. There's time for that later, but not at the beginning of the day. I personally believe that Twitter stands for Time Wasted In Trying To Escape Rejection. Social media is just a tool to help bring people to you (marketing) and give you a list of prospects (research).

There is certainly a vulnerable aspect in reaching out to people over the phone because at some point they can tell you "no." Just admit that you have some hesitation now and then. I certainly do. But action dissipates fear. So, before I open my email or get my coffee or even take my jacket off, I make one phone call. I open my database, find a warm prospect who loves me (not literally, of course), and call that person. Even if they are not in the office and you leave a voice mail, your action is pushing through that membrane of force that causes you to hesitate. If you don't believe me, test it for a week and see how much more effective you are. Once you make your dial, even if it results in a voice mail message, then give yourself permission to go get your coffee and open your email. Begin your day the way you want it to sustain itself over the next eight or nine hours, with action that leads to new business opportunities.

"And should you retain us, Mr. Hodal, you'll find that we're more than just a law firm."

SECRET #18

The Dirty Little Secret Why Rainmakers Need Therapy Skills

Rainmakers need therapy skills. Whether rainmakers need therapy is another topic.

Rainmakers need therapy skills because fear never sleeps. When clients hire professionals, there is always some fear in the background. Over the years many professionals we have interviewed shared this dirty little secret: a big part of a consulting engagement is acting like a therapist to the client.

We feel your pain. Often when we work with clients, we feel we could use some therapy skills.

One advantage of going to a licensed therapist is that you have a sounding board for what is bothering you; the same is true of a good professional. That is the view of Susan Zimmerman from Minneapolis.

Zimmerman, a financial consultant and licensed marriage and family therapist, has been a pioneer in blending finance and therapy for more than thirty years.

She is the author of five books, including *Mindful Money for Wealth and Well-Being: Help Clients Strike a Balance in Financial Planning*,[26] which was listed #1 in "Must-Reads for Advisers" by *Investment News* magazine.

Is it crazy to have expertise in both financial consulting and therapy? No, says Zimmerman, who believes it is not only sane, but also important and brilliant.

"Because it's never just about the numbers," says Zimmerman. "Numbers mean nothing without an understanding of how they can provide genuine, harmonious, and long-lasting solutions to human problems. And human problems are fraught with a multitude of emotions. Yes, even the money ones. Especially the money ones."

Zimmerman says it is not possible to separate emotions and logic, so the best bet for consultants is to fully embrace an understanding of both.

"There are 3,000 words for emotions in the English language," says Zimmerman. "Most people are only aware of a handful, especially when it comes to their money. But when they engage in therapeutically driven conversations from their life advisors, their elevated emotional intelligence makes all the difference in positive outcomes."

Therapeutic means to have a restorative effect. What is it that needs restoring when problems have surfaced and worsened? Zimmerman lists the following:

- Communication that's respectful and brings harmony back to relationships

- Confidence in one's ability to make sound financial decisions

- Willingness to look within and adjust old habits as needed

- Mindful awareness of psychological aspects of individual personality

"When consultants skillfully guide conversations therapeutically for optimal decision-making, clients experience prosperity clarity," says Zimmerman. "That's the magic that heightens their ability to identify profitable and satisfying choices, so they thrive through their life's purpose, leaving a lasting and meaningful legacy."

There are proven steps for success when it comes to listening carefully and responding appropriately to prospects and clients. First, identify what's on their mind. Why did they reach out to you? What are their goals, what assets do they have in place, and what are their roadblocks? Ask questions to find out and listen carefully. Then, to respond appropriately, match your language to the mindset of the prospect.

Here is how you bring a therapy best practice to consulting. During conversations with a prospect or client, we believe the goal of a consultant acting as a sounding board should be to monopolize the listening. Our rule of thumb is to listen 80 percent of the time and talk 20 percent.

MAKE IT RAIN

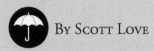 By Scott Love

First, identify your top five clients who have the highest likelihood of giving you more work. How often do you reach out to them currently? Depending on your business cycle, I think at least one contact a quarter for each past client would be a minimum contact.

Here are some ways you can keep in contact with this group of people in the area that is most likely to bear fruit. Sometimes just by your keeping top of mind with them, they will think of you for a business opportunity. "Thanks for reaching out. By the way, can we talk this week? We have a new potential matter that one of your colleagues may be able to help us with."

Here are some ideas in keeping top of mind with this first group of people.

The "I thought of you" message. Emails are easy, but not necessarily considered valuable contacts as it's too convenient and cheap to just send an email to say you were thinking of them. The message needs to be "I thought of you" plus offer value that does not translate into monetary reciprocation to you. It cannot be a hook into a pitch. It needs to be disconnected from your own selfish motive and the intention is merely to keep you top of mind. There are indeed times where you need to be more overt in your communication about getting work from a client, such as a major news story that could impact your client. "I saw this trend and felt we should reach out and assess your potential risk."

That's not what this is. This is a message that lets them know you are thinking of them but also has value that has nothing to do with your personal remuneration. You can do this by including an article about something that might be a solution to a problem that they have. When you do this, you need to include a personal note related to something that is nonbusiness. "Hope you and your wife and kids have a fun vacation this summer. By the way, I thought this article would be interesting to you."

The "Panel Opportunity" reach-out. If you see that your client is sitting on a panel for an industry conference, mention this. Find out about what he or she will be speaking about, where it is, and maybe you might be able to go.

The "In the News" reach-out. If you see that they have been mentioned in the news, congratulate them.

The Podcast Interview reach-out. You should be a guest on podcasts related to your expertise. If you are a guest on a show, send the link to the recording to all your existing clients. Say something like you were pleased with how it turned out and thought there would be some useful content in your interview that would benefit them. Remember it's all about the content and the value to them, not the ego boost for you.

The second path to new business is people who know you. These are those with whom you have never done business and who have never hired you. But there is a connection. It doesn't have to be a meaningful connection, but a legitimate connection. They may not even remember the connection taking place, but that doesn't matter. I've reached out to people who I had spoken with years ago, and they may not remember it. But when I reach out to them, I mention this, and it still opens the door.

When you speak with cold contacts, after you speak to them, you can move them to this second category. Each contact with someone whom you make, even if cold and a sale doesn't result from it, is valuable because moving them from category five to category two is a significant amount of movement. Therefore, all connections are valuable, not just those that result in a transaction.

The third path to new business is people who are referrals. Please reread the secrets on referrals.

The fourth path to new business is those who have heard of you. Therefore, we write, speak, get published, get quoted, and sit on panels at industry conferences.

The fifth path to new business is cold calls. In my business of recruiting partners, it's common for me to make cold reach-outs to partners with big law firms to tap them on the shoulder and make an introduction. But if I were to have that strategy for developing business, I would need to recognize that this is the least likely way to contact a new prospect. But there is an exception to this rule, and here are a few ideas on how you can at least harvest value with cold contacts. In short, there are two exceptions: solving immediate problems, and ego.

Solving immediate problems: Suppose you and I owned a fire extinguisher business. We would drive around our truck in the city looking for fires. If we saw a fire in a building, we would call the owner of the building and tell him that he has a fire on the third floor and that we are in the fire extinguisher sales business and we would ask if he wanted to buy fire extinguishers from us. He would respond, "Yes! I'll take twenty," and we would sell them to him and know that we made a sale using an effective strategy. This is how you can indeed make cold reach-outs. In some professional services, such as in law firms, it's a highly unlikely strategy. In other industries, such as the recruiting industry where a good placement solves a specific problem, then a cold call can work effectively.

Great Rainmaking Is Great Storytelling

If you want to attract high-paying clients, what insights can you give away for free and can you do it in story form? After all, humans are hardwired for stories.

"Marketing is storytelling, and great storytelling transcends languages and cultures."

That is advice from Ross Kimbarovsky on how to create content-marketing unicorns. Following a thirteen-year career as a successful trial attorney, in 2007 Kimbarovsky founded crowdspring, an online marketplace for crowdsourced creative services, where he serves as CEO.

In today's vernacular, unicorn is shorthand for something that is a rarity, and great content marketing is rare. Content marketing is creating and sharing online material that does not explicitly promote a product, service, or brand but is intended to stimulate interest.

To stimulate more interest in your brand, here are tips from Kimbarovsky that will help you create your own client-attracting content-marketing unicorns:

The best content is concise and easy to read. "People don't *read* marketing copy," says Kimbarovsky. "They *scan*. You need to get to the point. Fast. The way you organize your content and the words you choose are important. Edit ruthlessly." Kimbarovsky contends active voice is always better than passive voice. "Use active voice whenever possible. That's because active voice is easier to read and more concise than passive voice." He says to compare the following two examples:

Passive: *"A new iPhone was bought by the customer."*

Active: *"The customer bought a new iPhone."*

Both statements are correct. But the passive statement de-emphasizes the subject (the customer) in favor of the object (the product). When you're writing marketing copy, your goal should be to connect with the customer, not with the product. "And, importantly, active voice is nearly always more concise than passive voice," says Kimbarovsky.

Connect your content to your audience. "Stories help shape beliefs and also help people remember the things you want them to remember," says Kimbarovsky. "Stories are powerful because they can create a mythology around a brand. And it helps that people love to hear stories about themselves and about others."

SECRET #19

Grow Your Small Business Exponentially

In everyday speech, exponential growth means runaway expansion. Math class taught us that compound interest, population increase, or radioactive decay are all applications of exponential functions. Exponential growth is the opposite of slow and steady wins the race.

Justin Breen preaches the gospel of exponential growth.

"I started my company with zero business experience, didn't know what an LLC was, still don't know what S-Corp means, didn't know you had to pay taxes four times a year, and never had heard the word entrepreneur," says Breen. "Now I'm CEO of a global company that only works with the top-mindset businesses and brands in the world."

Breen is CEO of the PR firm BrEpic Communications and author of the bestselling book *Epic Business*.[27] He is an extremely active member of Entrepreneurs' Organization, Strategic Coach, Secret Knock, and ProVisors, and has an incredible global network of visionaries and exceptional businesses.

MAKE IT RAIN

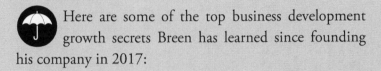 Here are some of the top business development growth secrets Breen has learned since founding his company in 2017:

Find your superpowers. "The main reason BrEpic has taken off faster than I could ever have possibly imagined is that I only do what I like to do best and what I'm good at. In other words, I focus entirely on my superpowers, which are connecting visionaries on a global level and earning clients major mainstream media appearances on a global level. I work exactly zero hours every week because none of this is work for me."

Partner with people who look at things as investments, not costs. "When someone asks what you charge or what do you cost within the first five to ten minutes of a conversation, it's an immediate disqualifier from being in my network or being a BrEpic client. That's because they are looking at things strictly in a transactional way—not in a relationship and/or partnership way. When someone asks: 'What does an investment with you and your firm look like,' this is music to my ears. There is a critical, vital difference between hearing the words cost versus investment."

Network equals net worth. "Having the right mindset attracts the right network. I only partner with people who have a visionary, investment, abundance mindset. Those are the folks who are running the top companies in the world, or the ones who will be one day. My company is essentially a giant incubator of geniuses with the right mindset, and they are constantly introducing me to others with an investment, visionary, abundance mindset."

Be a joiner. "Join ultra-high-level groups like Strategic Coach, Abundance 360, and Entrepreneurs' Organization: The three groups mentioned are among the top in the world. They include tens of thousands of visionaries—almost all of them look at things as investments, not costs, and almost all of them live in abundance, not scarcity. The groups weed out all the wrong-fit people and clients. When you are in groups, everything is collaborative, and entrepreneurs rise together."

Confidence is different from arrogance. "Top-level entrepreneurs are extremely confident in their superpowers. That attracts other confident people. Entrepreneurs are not arrogant or thinking they are great at everything. In fact, it's the exact opposite. They know they are actually not great at almost everything—I'm terrible at almost everything—and they either hire, outsource, or simply don't do everything they aren't exceptional at."

The bottom line for Breen is to embrace the future. "I'm a futurist, meaning things I said years ago are happening now."

"What's the fee we charge clients who call to complain about fees?"

SECRET #20

Avoid The Cult Of Overwork

Great business books by thought leaders share the why, the how and the what's next. You as reader supply the when.

Michael Hyatt is a rainmaking thought leader. If you want to attract high-paying clients, then his books like *Platform*[28] are a must. His latest book, a father-daughter effort to help achievers, *Win At Work Succeed At Life*, should be added to your reading list as soon as possible. The main message of the book is now is the time to free yourself from the cult of overwork.

Michael Hyatt and Megan Hyatt Miller know we can do better because the five principles in this book have revolutionized their professional achievements while supporting personal lives rich in meaning, relationships, and vitality.

"What concerns us most is the widely held assumption that you must abandon balance and sacrifice your personal wellness, family life, self-enrichment, emotional health, and spiritual wholeness just to be and stay competitive," they write in their book.

Backed by insights from psychology and organizational science and illustrated with eye-opening success stories from across the business spectrum and their own coaching clients, *Win at Work and Succeed at Life* is their manifesto on how you can achieve work-life balance and success.

Michael Hyatt is the founder and chairman of Michael Hyatt & Company. He has scaled multiple companies over the years, including a $250 million publishing company with 700-plus employees and his own leadership development company that has grown over 60 percent year over year for the last four years.

Megan Hyatt Miller is the president and chief executive officer of Michael Hyatt & Company. Cohost of the popular business podcast *Lead to Win*, she is also Michael's oldest daughter.

Most business book authors write a long book because they don't take the time to write a short one. At under two hundred pages, this book is a quick read, and can be digested in chunks. One of the positive attributes of this book is that it doesn't bite off too much for the reader to chew.

MAKE IT RAIN

Michael Hyatt and Megan Hyatt Miller want us to rethink a handful of ideas about work and productivity. The five principles covered in the book are:

Principle #1. Work is only one of many ways to orient your life. The book explores the idea of a double win: a perspective that sees work and life in partnership, not opposition. The authors admit it is never easy to draw new boundaries and renegotiate old deals, but it is necessary.

Principle #2. Constraints foster productivity, creativity, and freedom. The authors advise you to constrain your workday. Have barriers and boundaries. You are the boss of you.

Principle #3. Work-life balance is truly possible. Schedule what matters to you. One of the best practices is creating a profile of your ideal week. Every week is not ideal, but you should have a plan.

Principle #4. There is incredible power in nonachievement. Keep a hobby that delights you. This is something Gretchen Rubin also talked about in her landmark book *The Happiness Project.*

Principle #5. Rest is the foundation of meaningful, productive work. The authors ask us to rethink sleep. They state that "habitually shortchanging your sleep to meet deadlines, clear your inbox, or complete a project" is a shortsighted approach. Work and life are a marathon, not a sprint, and self-care is the investment that makes high achievement possible.

The bottom line: As Michael Hyatt and Megan Hyatt Miller state: "The cult of overwork is a powerful tide that can pull you far from shore if you're not aware of its force." Or to quote the closing line of F. Scott Fitzgerald's *The Great Gatsby*, "And so we beat on, boats against the current..."

"How do you want me to answer that question, Norm? As an attorney, or as your best friend?"

SECRET #21

Into The Rainmaking Future

Time to summarize the rainmaker confidential approach:

MAKE IT RAIN

Secret #1. Why Not Compare Your Rainmaking To Your Peers? Use the secrets of R&D (rob and duplicate) to succeed.

Secret #2. How The Best Rainmakers Invest Their Time, Treasure, And Talent. Remember the magnificent seven ways to make it rain.

Secret #3. Identify Client Motivations To Hire You. Seek first to understand what the prospect wants, not what you think they need.

Secret #4. Hone Your Personal Rainmaking Brand. Your personal brand must be memorable and stand for something.

Secret #5. Write Your Next Book Fast. The book is the number one rainmaking tool.

Secret #6. Speak Up, But Only If You Want To Make It Rain. The speech is the number one rainmaking strategy.

Secret #7. Attract Clients With Podcasts. Podcasts are the gift that keeps giving.

Secret #8. Make Relationships If You Want To Get Help Making It Rain. The real secret of success is it is all about relationships.

Secret #9. Use Key Influencers To Generate Word-Of-Mouth Advertising. Word-of-mouth advertising works so don't leave it to chance.

Secret #10. Monopolize The Listening. Follow the 80/20 rule for listening to the prospect versus speaking to the prospect.

Secret #11. How To Convert Prospects Into Clients. Fine-tune your prospect conversion process.

Secret #12. The Greatest Rainmaking Strategy In The World: Thought Leadership. Thought leaders do research and then type and talk about it.

Secret #13. Build A Network If You Don't Have One. Networks matter and you can rapidly build one from scratch.

Secret #14. Improve Your Voice Like Jeff, Gwen, Tony, And Angelina. Vocal power is a great strength for a rainmaker to have.

Secret #15. Consider A Side Hustle Like This One That Earned 40X ROI. You can leverage rainmaking into lucrative additional revenue streams.

Secret #16. Fire 90 Percent Of Your Clients. Firing wrong-fit clients makes room for right-fit clients.

Secret #17. Build A Rainmaker Culture. Culture trumps strategy and is a force multiplier for your rainmaking efforts.

Secret #18. The Dirty Little Secret Why Rainmakers Need Therapy. You need therapy skills to better deal with all those clients with problems.

Secret #19. Grow Your Rainmaking Exponentially. Just remember that network means net worth.

Secret #20. Avoid The Rainmaker Cult Of Overwork. Rainmaking is a marathon, not a 5K fun run.

The rainmakers who embrace the foregoing secrets will certainly attract a steady stream of high-paying clients. The results they receive will be in exact proportion to their focus, persistence, and desire to truly have impact and influence serving others.

Time To Plan A Strategic Rainmaking Retreat

According to one experienced strategic planning consultant and retreat facilitator, Scott Hamilton, a retreat is critical in these times "to keep your people actively engaged, to get their ideas and input, to get your people on the same page with where you are going, and to evolve your shared purpose, vision, and create a fresh, relevant strategy."

Hamilton, the CEO of NEXTWORKS Strategy of Irvine, California, has led many strategic planning retreats. He is a former corporate executive with DirecTV, Nestlé, Golden State Foods, and ARAMARK. As a strategy consultant he has supported the rapid growth of emerging companies in healthcare, med tech, and IT integration. He has also helped CEOs of declining sectors like printing, hospitality, and travel pivot to more profitable areas.

Hamilton is the leader of the Executive Next Practices Institute, which is located within UC Irvine Beall Applied Innovation, a campus-based incubator aimed at building ties between researchers, investors, and industry.

"Even before this COVID-19 crisis, the difficulty of a CEO and an executive team getting people on the same page was challenging," says Hamilton.

"There was often a significant misinterpretation between what they were saying and what people were hearing," says Hamilton. "So, the idea now is to communicate more with more intentionality and in a more two-way process. When people are truly engaged you can tap the collective intelligence of the organization. Now more than ever, it's critical to actually overcommunicate where you're going and how we're going to get there."

But does the formal nature of a strategic retreat over a platform like Zoom eliminate the ideas that came from the informal settings of the strategic retreat?

Typically, at an offsite retreat, participants spend all day in a room talking strategy. Then participants go to dinner and go out and play golf or have some other excursion. Hamilton sees great value in that out-of-the-room time.

"During those meals and excursions, you would have a sidebar conversation with someone, another member of your leadership team, and you'd come up with some great ideas based on reflection from the day's events," says Hamilton. "Those kinds of serendipitous ideas and creativity often are not possible in a virtual environment."

For retreats you can create opportunities for smaller groups to meet after the main session to talk about what they heard and start to ideate how they can move forward.

"So, you have to create these random collisions, if you will, in a virtual environment, just like you would see in a normal physical environment of a retreat," says Hamilton.

The bottom line: A rainmaking retreat must create a measurable impact. Here are two questions to guide you: Are you creating something that the rest of the organization can embrace? Will your clients recognize you as fresh and different?

Six Keys To Improve Your Virtual Rainmaking During A Pandemic And Beyond

What three results do all rainmakers want? The answer: more, cheaper, and faster.

Sure, the pandemic forced many to embrace that new-fangled virtual selling and long for the days of face-to-face sales. But is virtual rainmaking new?

"Many companies would have you believe virtual selling is new and constitutes a huge paradigm shift for them. But does it really?" asks author Craig Lowder. "Virtual selling has been around for over a hundred years; think catalogs, newspapers, direct mail offers, late-night TV infomercials, telemarketers, and e-commerce."

The difference now is the way that traditional outside sales teams interact with their buyers due to the pandemic and the need for social distancing.

Lowder, author of *Smooth Selling Forever*,[29] is a sales-effectiveness expert with a thirty-year track record of helping owners of small and midsize companies achieve their sales goals. As the president of MainSpring Sales Group, Lowder has worked with over fifty companies and increased first-year annual sales from 22 to 142 percent.

"Virtual selling is here to stay," says Lowder. "Expect it to grow exponentially over the coming years and decades. Both buyers and sellers are realizing unexpected benefits of virtual selling and buying."

MAKE IT RAIN

 According to Lowder, to become an effective virtual seller, consider six key building blocks:

Buyer Journey. "Everything starts with this. Changes in the buyer decision process will necessitate that sellers adjust their selling processes to accommodate the new buyer journey."

Messaging. "New digital sales support and marketing communication tools need to be created to gain the attention of, fully engage, and develop buyer relationships. Short and highly visual messages, including video, will be a must."

Meeting Cadence. "Virtual meetings in terms of their *length* (less than forty-five minutes), *frequency* (more often), and *pace* (fast) must be thoroughly grasped by sellers in order to connect with buyers."

Sales KPIs/Scorecards. "Sales key performance indicators, both activities and results, need to be attuned to a virtual selling environment."

Technology. "Virtual selling is reliant on a working knowledge of audio, visual, and lighting communications systems and tools in order to engage and build a relationship with buyers."

People. "The very people and communication skills they need to master are essential to effective virtual selling and require thorough scrutiny."

Here is why virtual rainmaking is here to stay. Buyers are benefiting from the ease in scheduling virtual meetings, shorter duration meetings, and a greater number of buying influences participating in virtual meetings. That results in both productivity gains and better decisions. Rainmakers are realizing similar benefits in the form of productivity gains, reduced selling costs, and in many cases, shorter sales cycles.

A Final Thought

When you follow these concepts and only put your time in areas that have a high likelihood of a favorable advantage, then you'll be able to turn what many might see as random chance into a predictable and highly probable business model.

May you have more high-paying clients, lower business development costs, and shorter times in your prospect pipeline. We wish you the best of all worlds: more, cheaper, and faster. Happy rainmaking.

APPENDIX A

Acknowledgments

The authors wish to express a great debt of gratitude to the many successful rainmakers who agreed to be a part of this research and are named in this book.

Henry DeVries

I wish to express gratitude for his many mentors who have recently passed: professor Glen Broom of San Diego State University, the world's leading public relations scholar, for four decades of mentoring and friendship; *Chino Champion* newspaper publisher Al McCombs, who gave me, at the age of fifteen, my first paying job as a writer; first coauthor Diane Gage Lofgren, who in 1990 taught me to be a coauthor; and professor Jack Douglass of UC San Diego, who in 1975 gladly took this teenager straight off a farm under his wing and taught me how to create the career of my dreams.

Also I want to thank the team at Indie Books International, including Mark LeBlanc, Ann LeBlanc, Vikki DeVries, Devin DeVries, Suzanne Hagen, Joni McPherson, Denise Montgomery, Jack DeVries, Don Sevrens, Sally Romoser, Heather Pendley, Taylor Graham, Adrienne Moch, Eric Gudas, Lisa Lucas, Jordan DeVries, and so many others who have helped me create my masterpiece: a business that is the Apple computer of consultant books, making it easy and affordable for every consultant to have more credibility, more impact, and more influence. To my Heavenly Father, thank you for helping me expand my territory so I can serve more of your children to get what they want in life. Thank you to the hundreds of authors, vendors, and investors who chose Indie Books International.

Scott Love

I wish to thank my many mentors along the way, such as Colonel Art Athens, USMC (ret), Major Thomas Love, USMC (ret), Vice Admiral Al Konetzni, USN (ret), Jim Vockley, Jeffrey Gitomer, the late Bill Brooks, Jeff Kaye, and Jeff Hayzlett. I also would like to thank my eleventh grade English teacher at Gregory-Portland High School, Mrs. Harris, for teaching me how to write to the ear, eliminate adverbs and adjectives, and use action verbs. Also, both Alan Weiss and Patricia Fripp have made a significant impact in my career, both in my work as a high-stakes headhunter and as a professional speaker. And finally, but not least, I express my heartfelt gratitude to my wife Darrah for being a supportive friend and life partner.

Mark LeBlanc

I have a deep well of mentors, friends, and clients who have shaped the way he thinks, makes decisions, acts, and celebrates his results. These include and are not limited to: Robert Rickey, Bob Thorson, Fr. Ken Opat, OSC, Gus Lactaoen, Mike McKinley, Bob Erickson, Dr. Lyman K. (Manny) Steil, Tim Gard, John Blumberg, Francis Bologna, Dr. John Givogre, Henry DeVries, Eleni Kelakos, Terri Langhans, Sherry Coauette, John LeBlanc, Kylie Strem, and so many more.

At twenty-one, when my employer suggested I did not have the work ethic to make it on my own, I vowed to do whatever it would take to be my own boss and make it on my own. I will soon celebrate my fortieth year of entrepreneurial success and achievements and have earned many accolades along the way. Last but not least, I wish to thank every single professional who trusted me, believed in my work, and attended one of my over two hundred business development retreats.

APPENDIX B

About The Authors

Henry DeVries writes a weekly business development column for Forbes.com and is the cohost of *The Marketing With A Book Podcast*. He is CEO of Indie Books International, has ghostwritten or edited more than three hundred business books, including his #1 Amazon sales and marketing bestseller, *How To Close A Deal Like Warren Buffett*. In his book and presentations titled "Persuade With A Story!" he shows thousands of professionals each year how to uncover hidden asset hero stories that communicate trustworthiness in two minutes or less. He earned his MBA from San Diego State University and a certificate in Leading Professional Service Firms from the Harvard Business School. On a personal note, he is a baseball nut who has visited forty-four major league baseball parks and has three to go before he can touch 'em all. He can be reached at henry@indiebooksintl.com. Learn more about Henry at his LinkedIn page: https://www. linkedin.com/in/ henryjdevries/ or by visiting the website for Indie Books International: http://indiebooksintl.com.

Scott Love is the host of *The Rainmaking Podcast* and is the founder of The Attorney Search Group, a legal recruiting firm that places rainmaking partners in global law firms and facilitates group and firm mergers. His perspective as a front-line expert on rainmaking and client development has led to quotes and mentions in the *Wall Street Journal, Forbes, Bloomberg, Huffington Post, Selling Power Magazine, The American Lawyer, Above The Law*, and dozens of business publications around the globe. Scott speaks professionally to all types of business and association groups on the topics of sales performance and client development and is a member of The National Speakers Association. He is a graduate of the United States Naval Academy in Annapolis, Maryland, and is a former Surface Warfare Officer. Learn more about Scott at his LinkedIn page https://www.linkedin.com/in/scotttlove/. Learn more about his podcast at http://www.therainmakingpodcast.com.

Mark LeBlanc, CSP, runs a speaking business based in Minneapolis, Minnesota. He conducts presentations and creates retreat-type experiences for independent and practice professionals who want to create an extreme sliver of focus and put more money in their pocket. He is the cohost of *The Marketing With A Book Podcast*. His nationally renowned *Achievers Circle* business retreat is ideal for professionals who want to develop a path and plan for true business growth. In fact, he has authored or coauthored five business development books, including his underground bestseller *Growing Your Business*. He has given over one thousand presentations and conducted over two hundred business retreats. Mark is a past president of the National Speakers Association and was inducted into the Minnesota Speakers Hall of Fame in 2006. He can be reached at Mark@ GrowingYourBusiness.com. Learn more about Mark at his LinkedIn page: https://www.linkedin.com/in/speaker-mark-leblanc-89b311/ or his website at: www.MarkLeBlanc.com

APPENDIX C

Schedule A Rainmaker Retreat

I f you would be open to a conversation about a Rainmaker Retreat for your firm, please reach out to Henry DeVries, Scott Love, or Mark LeBlanc. In these uncertain times, there is something all professional service firms need right now: *more clients.*

Ideally, retreats take place with a three-hour Thursday afternoon session, a Thursday networking dinner, and then two three-hour sessions and a lunch on a Friday. Here is who to contact:

MAKE IT RAIN

 Henry DeVries specializes in retreats for accounting, marketing and advertising, and technology services firms.

Scott Love specializes in retreats for law firms and other types of professional services firms.

Mark LeBlanc specializes in retreats for dental consultants, financial services, and management consulting firms.

There are a handful of variables that determine the cost of the Rainmaker Retreat, which we are happy to talk you through during the conversation.

The new normal is not normal for a professional service firm; it is more like trying to find clients on a burning platform. For thirty years the metaphor of a burning platform has symbolized an intense level of urgency for change, but it has never been more true. These are urgent times and to connect with clients and become influential, your professional service firm needs to be rainmaker storytellers who can attract clients, land accounts, and cement client relationships—all without necessarily being face-to-face with prospects.

Find out what you need to know and what you need to do to take your firm up one level, or four. As business development experts we share nine best practices around rainmaking, including insider strategies, steps, and tools for making it happen in the new normal. These days there is one hidden asset that will set you apart, something nobody else is offering: *your defining stories.* Together let's mine those hidden asset stories.

APPENDIX D

Other Books By The Authors

Other Books by Henry DeVries:

Self-Marketing Secrets (with Diane Gage)

Pain-Killer Marketing (with Chris Stiehl)

Client Seduction (with Denise Montgomery)

Closing America's Job Gap (with Mary Walshok and Tappan Monroe)

Marketing the Marketers

How to Close a Deal Like Warren Buffett (with Tom Searcy)

Marketing with a Book

Persuade with a Story!

Client Attraction Chain Reaction

Build Your Consulting Practice (with Mark LeBlanc)

Defining You (with Mark LeBlanc and Kathy McAfee)

Persuade With A Case Acceptance Story! (with Penny Reed and Mark LeBlanc)

Persuade With A Digital Content Story! (with Lisa Apolinski)

Other Books By Scott Love:

Why They Follow: How to Lead with Positive Influence

The Recruiters Adventure Book: How to Find Buried Treasure in the World of Recruiting

Scott Love's Weekly Recruiting Tips eBook

Other Books By Mark LeBlanc:

Growing Your Business

Never Be The Same

Build Your Consulting Practice (with Henry DeVries)

Defining You (with Kathy McAfee and Henry DeVries)

Persuade With A Case Acceptance Story! (with Penny Reed and Henry DeVries)

APPENDIX E

Notes

1   Tom Searcy and Henry DeVries, *How To Close A Deal Like Warren Buffett* (New York: McGraw-Hill, 2013).

2   Michael Zipursky, *ACT NOW: How Successful Consultants Thrive* (Vancouver, Consulting Success, 2020).

3   Ben Mezrich, *Bringing Down The House* (New York: Atria Books, Simon & Schuster, 2003).

4   Jeffrey Gitomer, *Little Red Book of Selling* (Portland: Bard Press, 2004).

5   Jim Kaspari, *PEAK Profits* (Sacramento: Jim Kaspari, 2019).

6   "Brand Intimacy COVID Study," MBLM (The Brand Intimacy Agency), https://mblm.com/lab/covid/

7   Judy Carter, *The Message of You* (New York: St. Martin's Press, 2013).

8   Judy Carter, *The Comedy Bible* (New York: Fireside, Simon & Schuster, 2001).

9   Ken Blanchard and Spencer Johnson, *The New One Minute Manager* (New York: William Morrow, 2015).

10 Henry DeVries and Diane Gage, *Self-Marketing Secrets* (San Diego: Pfeiffer,1991).

11 Roger Bolton, "Remembering Diane Gage Lofgren," Arthur W, Page Society. PAGETURNER (blog), January 25, 2021. http://page.org/blog/remembering-diane-gage-lofgren.

12 Minal Sampat, *Why Your Marketing Is Killing Your Business* (Washington State: Minal Sampat, 2020).

13 Debbie Peterson, *CLARITY* (Cape Coral: Debbie Peterson, 2019).

14 Doug Sandler, The Sandler Selling System, https://www.sandler.com/sandler-selling-system/.

15 ENP Institute, Executive Next Practices Institute, https://www.enpinstitute.com/. (Scott Hamilton is also CEO of NEXTWORKS Strategy, as mentioned in Secret #21.)

16 Mark LeBlanc, Kathy McAfee, and Henry DeVries, *Defining You* (Oceanside: Indie Books International, 2019).

17 Bryan Gray, Jesse Laffen, Paul Davison, and Mike Rendel, *The Priority Sale* (Oceanside: Indie Books International, 2021).

18 Mahoney & Zaltman, "The Subconscious Mind of the Consumer (And How To Reach It)," *Harvard Business Review*, Jan 13, 2003.

19 Joe Pallo, *How To Sell Nothing* (Oceanside: Indie Books International, 2021).

20 Jim Horan, *The One Page Business Plan* (Berkeley: The One Page Business Plan Company, 2006).

21 Robert Sher, *Mighty Midsized Companies* (London: Routledge, 2016).

22 Harvey Mackay, *Dig Your Well Before You're Thirsty* (New York: Currency, The Crown Publishing Group,1999).

23 Arthur Samuel Joseph, *Vocal Leadership* (New York: McGraw-Hill, 2014).

24 Nic Bittle, *Good Foreman; Bad Foreman* (Corn: Gold Standard Press, 2016).

25 Nic Bittle, *Know This; Do That* (Corn: Gold Standard Press, 2018).

26 Susan Zimmerman, *Mindful Money Matters* (Minneapolis: Mindful Asset Planning, 2017).

27 Justin Breen, *Epic Business* (Hayward: RHG Media Productions, 2020).

28 Michael Hyatt, *Platform* (Nashville: Thomas Nelson, 2012).

29 Craig Lowder, *Smooth Selling Forever* (Oceanside: Indie Books International, 2016).

APPENDIX F

Index

Made in the USA
Middletown, DE
21 December 2021

55667168R00109